A year ago, I'd been sitting in another restaurant like this, in despair and with nowhere to go. It had felt like my life held no joy. I'd clenched my trembling hands and leaned forwards to try and peer into the turbulent river, and then I'd tumbled in and been swept away, onwards and onwards, gripped by the powerful current; and when I came round, I found I had been washed up here, and I could no longer recall that place I'd left behind.

brazen

READERS LOVE IT

'Very beautiful, very honest and very good.'

'This is a special one.'

'If you like books, you'll love this one.'

'A love letter to reading . . . Cosy, cute and healing.'

'A memoir that goes down like a novel.'

'Fascinating . . . Both quirky and captivating.'

'A beautiful, thought-provoking memoir that will stick with me.'

'I found it really hard to put down and could have easily finished it in one sitting.'

'It's even better than "healing fiction" because it's not fiction.'

'This book made my heart sing.'

'This was SO GOOD!'

'I can't recommend it enough.'

'Fantastic . . . I looked up most of the books she recommended.'

'Understated, entertaining and beautifully narrated . . . Stunning.'

'A real hidden gem.'

'I'm all for books that lead you to more books.'

THE BOOKSHOP WOMAN

NANAKO HANADA

TRANSLATED BY CAT ANDERSON

brazen

First published in Great Britain in 2024 by Brazen,
an imprint of Octopus Publishing Group Ltd
Carmelite House, 50 Victoria Embankment, London, EC4Y 0DZ
www.octopusbooks.co.uk

An Hachette UK Company
www.hachette.co.uk

The authorized representative in the EEA is Hachette Ireland,
8 Castle Court Centre, Dublin 15, D15 XTP3, Ireland (email: info@hbgi.ie)

First published in paperback in 2025

Copyright © Nanako Hanada 2018
Translation copyright © Cat Anderson 2024
Design & illustration copyright © Octopus Publishing Group Ltd 2024

All rights reserved. No part of this work may be reproduced or utilised
in any form or by any means, electronic or mechanical, including
photocopying, recording or by any information storage and retrieval
system, without the prior written permission of the publisher.

Nanako Hanada has asserted her right under the Copyright, Designs and
Patents Act 1988 to be identified as the author of this work.

Cat Anderson has asserted her right under the Copyright, Designs and
Patents Act 1988 to be identified as the translator of this work.

ISBN 978-1-91424-078-2

eISBN 978-1-91424-079-9

A CIP catalogue record for this book is available from the British Library.

Printed and bound in Great Britain.

1 3 5 7 9 10 8 6 4 2

This FSC® label means that materials used
for the product have been responsibly sourced.

MIX
Paper | Supporting
responsible forestry
FSC® C104740

CONTENTS

Prologue	January 2013, midnight, rock bottom	1
Chapter 1	Tokyo is an open door	7
Chapter 2	I love you, Village Vanguard	39
Chapter 3	Life starts to move	55
Chapter 4	People in transit	89
Chapter 5	Unsolicited advice (among other things)	109
Chapter 6	Facing the final boss	135
Chapter 7	Sorry, Grandpa	155
Epilogue	Endings and beginnings	181
Afterword	Autumn 2017, in a bookshop	199

Books recommended in this book	207
Books recommended for people who've read this book	211

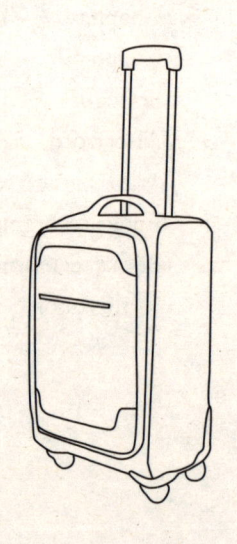

PROLOGUE

JANUARY 2013, MIDNIGHT, ROCK BOTTOM

I'm sitting alone in a family restaurant on the outskirts of Yokohama, numbly waiting for 2am. At times like these, I can't even bring myself to open a book. On the chair next to me is the suitcase I've been taking to work, into which I've stuffed the clothes I need for the foreseeable future, plus a few other necessities. For a week now, I've been homeless.

Tonight I'm planning to stay at a nearby super sento, one of those big public bathhouses with plenty of facilities where you can sleep in a lounge chair. It costs extra if you stay more than six hours, though, which makes things awkward: to keep the cost down to three thousand yen, I have to check in after two in the morning. I've been choosing my accommodation based on whether I need to get a good night's sleep, do my laundry or really economise. Depending on the priority, I stay in a cheap room somewhere, a super sento or a capsule hotel.

Every day, once evening comes, I have to start looking for somewhere to spend the night. Living this way is wearying.

It drains me to see my hard-earned money disappear on accommodation each day. How long can I keep this up?

'We can't go on living together like nothing's happened. Tomorrow I'm going to work, and I won't be coming home.' So I said to my husband a week ago, before I left our flat. I had nowhere in particular to go, no ideas about what to do next. And I hadn't left hoping it would change the way he felt, either.

I sip my coffee, which is now stone cold, and churn things over in my mind. As miserable as this way of life is, I'm still undecided about what to do and I'm nowhere near wanting to return to our shared home. *I'll probably never go back*, I think. No. It's time to look for a new place. I'll live by myself, and get my life back on track.

I wonder whether people will pity me because my marriage has broken down. I don't want that. If I let it become part of my identity, it'll turn into a self-fulfilling prophecy, and I'll only end up making myself feel worse and worse. I don't want to spend my life feeling sorry for myself.

Until now, however, I've always spent my days off with my husband. If I'm on my own, what will I do with my free time? I'm the manager of a branch of Village Vanguard, one of a chain of shops selling books and assorted knick-knacks. Maybe it's because of my work, but my only hobbies are reading and visiting bookshops – of course I have no friends to spend my time off with. *My life is so lacking. I have nothing of my own.*

JANUARY 2013, MIDNIGHT, ROCK BOTTOM

My life is so lacking... I feel like I want to see things I've never seen before. To put myself out there, become a new me, a happy me.

In the end, that mentally exhausting period of homelessness didn't last very long. Before too long, I talked it over with my husband and we decided to give up the lease on our flat and go our separate ways. He left first. I found myself a cramped flat on the edge of the Tokyo sprawl, ten minutes' walk from Yokohama Station and close to work.

The oversized fridge that we'd bought when we got married dominated my tiny one-person kitchen. The view from my window was new and unfamiliar, but I still couldn't get excited about it. Cars streamed past endlessly on the main road outside. I would gaze at them vacantly and tell myself that things were going to get better soon, that the needle of my life was going to swing from negative back to zero – a fresh start.

*

It was just after the move that I found out about an intriguing people-matching site that I'll call 'PerfectStrangers'. I'd been skimming through a new book by a young social entrepreneur when something caught my eye. The author was discussing a new generation of online services, and among them was one that bore the tagline 'Spend just half an hour chatting to someone new.'

I knew straight away that this might be what I needed. I put down the book and reached for my phone.

*

PerfectStrangers required you to create an account, and to verify your identity using Facebook before you could log in. I'd never felt up to using social media and had avoided joining anything until now, so first I'd have to sort out an account with this Facebook thing.

Account registration, profile setup, verification, more account registration, more profile setup . . . After a lengthy process, I was finally able to browse the matching site. Staring back at me was a huge array of faces, headshot after headshot, each accompanied by a brief comment, such as 'Happy to talk jobs, hobbies or whatever you like. Let's chat!' or 'Hoping to exchange info with people who've started their own business, or are thinking about it.' And these people were inviting me to meet them – on such and such a day, at such and such a time, in Shibuya, in Shinjuku – 'Looking forward to talking to you!'

What on earth is this? I thought. I'd never seen anything like it.

It definitely resembled a dating site, but it didn't seem too iffy, maybe because it wasn't just aimed at meeting members of the opposite sex for romance. It looked quite upmarket, even – very different from my mental image of this kind of thing. Students, older gents, beautiful young women who looked like secretaries, salarymen, people who seemed like they'd probably ride round

JANUARY 2013, MIDNIGHT, ROCK BOTTOM

the city on expensive bicycles . . . They were all on this site, and they all existed out there somewhere in real life.

So, if I wanted to, I could meet any one of them in person? It sounded pretty incredible. But when I browsed the faces again wondering who to pick, it was harder than I'd expected. People who didn't have any particular hook in their profiles, who just said they were happy to talk about anything, failed to pique my interest. I was more inclined to meet the people who had some specific talking point, something you'd think might be hard to get excited about – the profiles that said things like 'I want to talk about love!' or 'I'm researching the brain!'

With this in mind, what would I write in my own profile? I could play it safe with something like 'My hobby is reading' or 'I'd like to talk about books.' But on this site it felt like that would leave such a non-impression, it would amount to writing nothing at all.

Wait. What about . . . ?

An idea popped into my head, but I quickly dismissed it. *You can't try that with people you've only just met. It's too out there. You've never done anything like that before.*

And yet it wouldn't matter if I failed. Even if I couldn't deliver what I promised, it would only result in a little disappointment for people. And it was better than nothing.

After much deliberation, I edited my profile and hit 'Save'. It now read: 'I'm the manager of a very unusual bookshop. I have access to a huge database of over ten thousand books, and I'll recommend the one that's perfect for you.'

I still wasn't sure if this was a good idea. But there it was.

And so, armed with only an untested idea for a weapon, I ventured out onto the mysterious matching site. My journey had begun.

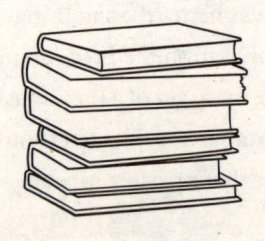

CHAPTER 1

TOKYO IS AN OPEN DOOR

'Ah, you must be Nanako?' the tall man said as soon as he entered the café. He looked like he was in his early forties, and had a calmer, more relaxed vibe than I was expecting.

'I'm Tsuchiya. Nice to meet you,' he said as he sat down in front of me, cool and collected. 'Have you already ordered something to drink? I come here a lot; they do very good cheesecake. Would you like to try some? Go on, it really is delicious – let me treat you to a piece.'

It was an occasion worth commemorating. My encounter with Tsuchiya, my very first PerfectStrangers match.

*

After I'd registered my profile on PerfectStrangers, I perused the site until I understood how it worked. It looked like there were two ways to meet someone. You set a time and approximate location (say, 5pm on such and such a day, in Shibuya), added a short comment ('Looking forward to a great chat!') and then posted it on the site. This was known as 'listing a chat'.

Logged-in users could view these listings on a notice board, and if they wanted to meet you, they could reply to your post by clicking 'Respond'. If you received multiple responses, you sifted through them and picked the person you most wanted to meet. If you didn't feel like meeting any of them, you could decline them all and cancel the listing. And if you didn't get any responses, of course, your meeting would just fall through. So in order to meet someone, you had to either list a chat and wait for someone to respond, or respond to someone else's listing.

Just making a profile wasn't enough to set things in motion. The more I browsed the site, the more I understood that, unlike Facebook or Twitter, there was no fun in just browsing. All you could really do was 'like' the intriguing people at the top of the popularity rankings, or go through and tag all your interests – *#reading*, *#travel* and so on – and then check out people with the same tags as you.

I looked at the current listings by those who were seeking someone to meet. They were offering meetings at a whole range of different times, yet lots of them hadn't had a single response, their posts going unanswered. What if no one responded to mine either? That would be sad, embarrassing. Or what if I only got responses from weirdos? I dithered, unable to muster the resolve to set up my own meeting.

Just then, I got an alert from Facebook Messenger. I didn't recognise the sender.

'Hello! 👋 I'm Tsuchiya,' began the message, complete with friendly waving emoji. 'I work in advertising. I saw you on

PerfectStrangers and thought I'd message. I see you're new – nice to make your acquaintance! I'm not an expert, but if you need any help using the site, just ask. ☆'

I had mixed feelings. I was partly reassured by the appearance of this kind stranger, but also a little suspicious as to why he had contacted me out of the blue.

'Thank you for the offer. How did you find me, though?' I replied.

'Do you mean how I found you on Facebook? 😅' came the reply, accompanied by another emoji – this one looking slightly sheepish, I thought. The message continued, 'User profiles on PerfectStrangers have little Facebook and Twitter icons at the bottom. You can click them to see the user's Facebook or Twitter feed. If you get a response from someone you think might be dodgy, you should check out their social media – it can be good to see where they work and find out a bit more about them. You can tell more about what they're like from their posts and tweets, too.

'Also, people who've just signed up to PerfectStrangers and users who're currently online are displayed as featured users. Down at the bottom. Can you see that?'

It was pretty forward of him to message me like this, but at least he seemed friendly.

'Oh yes, I see it . . . Thanks for your help. It's all new to me,' I replied.

'Are you planning to list a chat? Or just looking around for now?' he asked.

'I guess nothing's going to happen till I list one. But I was worried no one would respond.'

'Why don't I be your first meeting then? If you set a date and time, I'll respond to your listing. You could set it up now for practice, if you want. It's always good to try new things! 🎵'

I felt a bit like I was being pushed into it, but then again, there was no point just staring at the site forever. This guy seemed all right, so why not meet up with him just to try it out?

'Okay, thank you. Let's give it a shot. I'll try posting now.'

And that was how my meeting with Tsuchiya came about.

Tsuchiya picked a place in Tokyo's Oku-Shibuya district, a stylish café that was serious about its coffee. I arrived first and waited, feeling jittery and nervous. *I'm about to socialise with a stranger! This is happening!* I kept glancing around the café and fidgeting, smoothing out the creases in my skirt.

But when Tsuchiya came in and we said hello, I found myself calming down and thinking that actually, this wasn't so scary after all. He was easy to talk to, which helped. By the time I'd ordered a coffee and a piece of the cheesecake he recommended, my nerves had all but disappeared.

'So . . . you've been using PerfectStrangers for quite a while, then?' I asked Tsuchiya. 'What made you decide to try it? How are you finding it?'

'Well, it makes a nice change from going for coffee on your own. And it's stimulating talking to young people, it sometimes gives me new ideas for work. It's good fun. What about you, why are you on the site?'

'I've separated from my husband. I thought it would be good to try something new, and I thought I might as well get some practice recommending books to people while I'm at it,' I said.

'You're separated? I see, you must've had a hard time of it then. I have a feeling I'm missing part of the story, though . . . You intrigue me, Nanako. Could I ask why you and your husband split up? It's absolutely fine if you don't want to talk about it.'

'Um . . .' I hesitated a moment.

My husband and I worked for the same company and we had a lot of friends in common, so I hadn't really spoken to anyone about our reasons for separating. If I only gave my side of the story, I'd inevitably sound like the victim, which didn't seem fair. I saw our separation as a mutual failure, and I had no desire to direct any blame or resentment towards my husband. In fact, I felt bad that the only conclusion I'd come to so far was that I wanted to put some space between us for a while, as a way of putting off the problem for the time being.

But Tsuchiya had no involvement in my life whatsoever. I didn't have to worry about him meddling – he wouldn't gossip to anyone who knew my husband, or tell my husband what I'd said. He was a total stranger who I'd be with today and today only, so I felt able to relax and even joke about the separation.

Tsuchiya listened with interest as I spoke, nodding attentively now and then.

'Well, you meet all sorts of people on the site!' he said. 'Seeing as you're separated, you could even use it to find a boyfriend. I mean, forgive me for saying this – but a person can miss that physical connection, don't you think?'

Um, excuse me? I was taken aback by his misguided words of encouragement. But then it occurred to me that maybe in a situation like this, people felt they could be more familiar, and mention things like sex more easily.

'Oh, I'm not really missing the physical connection. But I suppose it might be nice to find a boyfriend some time,' I said noncommittally, trying to sidestep the topic.

But Tsuchiya continued. 'I mean, not *connection*, exactly, but . . . Well, I'm talking about sexual intimacy! Though I thought that might be too blunt. But it's not particularly outrageous to suggest that women might want sex too, is it?'

For some reason, our discussion seemed to assume that I was sexually frustrated.

'That's just how it is,' Tsuchiya continued, as though pressing me for some kind of acknowledgement. 'I mean, I'm a great believer in equality between men and women, I respect women. But women who try so hard on their own without a man can seem a bit . . . you know? I think a woman can really blossom when she's got a man to love and fulfil her.'

'Oh . . .?' I said. I realised I was smiling through gritted teeth. This seemed to be a pet theory of his – and a totally antiquated one at that.

'Don't get me wrong, I'm not trying to say you always need a man around, or that you look desperate or anything like that! I just meant, I'm sure you'll find someone.'

'Thank you very much. Yes – it would be lovely if I could find a nice man like Pierre Taki,' I said, trying to wrest the baton from Tsuchiya and change the subject.

'Pierre Taki? What, the actor? Is he your type? That's unusual! Well, I may not be as entertaining as him, but I'll go out for dinner with you any time, and you can talk about how things are with your husband, or whatever's bothering you, and get it all off your chest. Sex or no sex, it's fine by me – your wish is my command. Only kidding!'

So, he wanted to steer the conversation back to sex after all. I was getting fed up – but I couldn't deny that it was thanks to Tsuchiya I'd taken this first step. I should really be much obliged to him.

'That's very nice of you, but I think at the moment I just want to try meeting lots of different people on PerfectStrangers. It's been great meeting you like this, so I'm really excited to meet other people too!' I answered, mentally adding, *by which I mean, I don't plan on seeing you again.*

'Yes. Of course. It's just there are a lot of dodgy people on there,' he said. At this point it was probably time to tell him to have a good long look in the mirror.

'Well, they can't be much dodgier than you,' I said, jokingly rebuffing him.

'Hey! That's a terrible thing to say! Come on now, let's be friends,' he said, getting into the spirit of things.

'Hmm . . . Nah, seems too much like hard work.'

'Oh, too mean!'

I found it refreshing that in this thirty-minute slot I'd been able to drop all formality and poke fun at him, that we'd been able to trade jests. And the fact I wouldn't have to see him again made it easier, somehow.

My gentle snub seemed to have done the trick, and after that Tsuchiya chatted to me about the ad industry, what his job involved and the adverts he'd worked on recently, as far as he could discuss them.

As our meeting was coming to its end, I hastily asked him about books. What kind of thing did he usually read, and what might he like to try?

'Well, I haven't read that much recently . . . Maybe a novel?' he said.

From what I gathered, he didn't keep up with the latest books or read an awful lot. To be honest, I'd been put off by that doggedness of his, often found in middle-aged men: his pushing for another meeting and attempting to crowbar in the subject of sex. But he showed some sensitivity when he talked about his work, and I felt there was a more nuanced side to him. Based on his personality and his job, I thought he'd probably like to read something contemporary, rather than a classic.

I would recommend him something by Takehiro Higuchi, an author I'd discovered just recently and been blown away by.

When I'd first read Higuchi's writing, I was thrilled – he used language in a totally new way and presented such a fresh perspective. Tsuchiya worked in advertising, after all, so if he wasn't already familiar with this new talent, I would introduce him. *Farewell Zoshigaya* would be a great choice . . . But then, Tsuchiya seemed to have sex on the brain, so instead I picked *Sex in Japan*. It was right there in the title, so maybe he'd give the book a shot. It was suitably current, too, having just come out in paperback.

Sex in Japan is about a husband and wife who venture into the world of swinging. At first it just seems like a piece of erotica, but midway through it becomes a novel about violence, and then a court-room novel, and it finishes up as a story about pure love. It's entertaining in its absurdity, a real rollercoaster of a ride. I hoped Tsuchiya would enjoy it.

So that was how I made my first book recommendation. I sent it to Tsuchiya a day or two later via Facebook Messenger, along with a few words of thanks.

*

Meeting a stranger had been less scary than I'd expected. What's more, I'd been down in the dumps recently because of the separation and work, but when I met Tsuchiya, with his complete lack of involvement in my problems, I'd found myself feeling cheerful and happy for the first time in a long while. Another side of myself had surfaced, one that wasn't completely weighed down by my current predicament. Even I was a little surprised.

Encouraged by this initial success, I tried listing my own chat the very next day. It so happened that I didn't have work, so I had gone into Tokyo. When it got to the evening, I decided to post on PerfectStrangers in the spirit of a casual experiment. If I listed a spontaneous meeting starting in just an hour's time, would anyone see it and respond?

Ten minutes passed with no replies. I supposed people didn't necessarily check the site that frequently, and it was unlikely anyone would be free at such short notice. I was just about to give up when I received a response. It was from someone called Koji.

'I saw your listing. I'd love to meet up! I'm at work right now and I finish soon, but I probably won't manage 8. What about 8.30-ish?'

Before replying, I checked Koji's profile. He seemed to have met quite a few people already; their comments said things like, 'A cheerful, interesting guy,' 'We got so into our conversation we ended up staying way longer haha,' and 'He's so positive and full of energy!'

Okay, so he seemed fine.

'No worries. I'll be in the café reading. Just take your time,' I replied.

And so I was all set for my next meeting. Koji – my second match.

I read a book as I waited for him. The café was a retro place that harked back to the Showa era. It was very quiet, and I was just wondering if it would be a good place to chat or whether it would be awkward, when I got a new message.

'Really sorry, work dragged on! Just leaving, will be there around 9.10.'

To tell the truth, I was slightly irritated. So now we were meeting more than an hour after originally planned? I could have spent that time with someone else, but now it had been completely wasted. And anyway – why did I have to fit around his schedule? But then again, if I really didn't want to hang around, all I had to do was message and say, 'Okay, guess it's off then!' So I let go of my irritation – after all, there was no real need for me to get home early. I'd got this far, so I might as well meet the guy.

However, the café closed at nine, so it would have to be somewhere else. There were no other cafés in the area open this late, and I was hungry, so I told Koji I'd be waiting at a nearby bar and sent him a link. It would be stupid to wait around only to be disappointed again, so I was going to get myself something to eat and drink.

'Are you Nanako? Sorry, sorry, sorry! I'm really sorry!'

The man who appeared in front of me was around thirty. He had a vigorous, healthy look about him: a sporty type, maybe, with his loud voice and excitable energy. I couldn't help smiling at his apology, which was so overblown I suspected he didn't really feel bad at all.

'Oh, don't worry about it. I just got myself some pizza,' I said.

'Ah, you're smiling! What a relief! That makes me feel much better, it really does. Mmm, pizza sounds good, I'm hungry too! What kind of pizza is it? Have you got room for more? Let's go big today – let's eat, let's drink! I'll treat you, to say sorry for being late!'

He took a seat at the bar and turned his rapid-fire chatter on the barman.

'Two beers please! The biggest glasses you've got! A keg, if you have one! Oh, you only have steins? That's okay! Not a problem!'

We raised our glasses to each other and then he finally settled down long enough to start a conversation.

'So, Nanako. You've only just joined PerfectStrangers, haven't you? I feel very privileged to meet you today,' he said.

'It's nice to meet you too. You've met quite a few people already, then?' I asked.

'Oh, well – yes, I suppose . . .' he said, scratching his head bashfully for some reason.

'How come you're on PerfectStrangers?' I asked him.

'Right now I work for a start-up in children's education, but I'd like to start my own business at some point, so I'm saving money while I work on my ideas,' said Koji. 'I've always worked in education, so if I do go for it, it'll probably be in the same sort of field. But the company I'm working for at the moment is all men and there's no opportunity to get a woman's perspective. I'm using PerfectStrangers to share my ideas and solicit opinions!' He rattled all this off briskly as though conscious of making a good impression, like a recent graduate at an interview who'd been asked why he'd applied for the job.

'Oh, okay. I can see people use the site in lots of different ways, then!' I said.

Koji asked me why I'd decided to sign up, so I briefly revisited the things I'd talked about with Tsuchiya yesterday. He listened, giving great exaggerated nods and frowns and smiles.

'That's amazing! So you're taking on a new challenge! And I get to be here at this pivotal point in your life. Gosh, I feel very grateful. Maybe it's fate that I got to meet you today, to see you moving forward with such positivity. Your attitude inspires me to try harder. You have my absolute, full support!' he said. For some reason, he was proffering me a handshake. It seemed whatever Koji said – the actual merit of his words aside – he always gave it 110 per cent.

'Oh, er . . . thanks.' I extended my hand to shake his, despite feeling a slight urge to pull back.

'Oh no! I'm annoying you, aren't I? I'm coming on too strong! I can tell, I've lived with this personality for thirty years. I'm used to people thinking that about me!' he said.

'No, no, I'm just not used to it! Sorry, I'll probably warm up once we get to know each other better,' I said.

'So you feel cold towards me? Even worse! No, it's true, I can tell! But words are powerful, so I always feel like I should keep talking! I really meant it when I said I was grateful, there's no point being shy about that stuff. See? I just have to keep putting things into words! I want to be positive, like – like a wild animal, charging forward to face any challenge. Like So Takei, you know? The athlete? No? What, *really?* But anyway, Nanako – you're so beautiful! You really, really, really are!'

'What? I—What?'

Koji was exhausting, but he wasn't necessarily a bad person. I couldn't quite match his enthusiasm, needless to say, but he seemed to have an extraordinary power, because just by talking with him I found myself growing more cheerful. In the end, I was overwhelmed by his strange energy and I stayed for another drink. We ended up chatting for a whole two hours.

When I asked Koji about books, he said, 'I want to know what makes you tick, Nanako' (he'd become very familiar with me, even though I was older). 'Which book are you most into right now, or which one will help me understand you better? I promise I'll get a copy and read it!'

I felt somewhat deflated by this, but I supposed that was one way of getting to know someone. I'd have to have a think about it when I got home.

Which book was I most into right now?

In the end, I decided to introduce Koji to *Telling You How I Feel: The Complete Exhibition* by the artist Ellie Omiya. The book was a record of a solo exhibition Ellie had put on, told through photos and writing. It might not be that interesting to someone who wasn't already into her work, but it was what I'd been reading throughout my spell of homelessness, which had ended only a few days before. The book was like my lucky charm, and I'd opened it again and again and cried every time. It meant so much to me. I was deeply moved by Ellie's message about the importance of trying to connect with people even though it was such a hard thing to do, and if her words touched Koji, too, I would be very happy. I wrote my recommendation and sent it to him via Facebook Messenger.

Koji's reply came quickly.

'Thanks for the book recommendation, Nanako! I had such a great evening! It's hard to explain, but I felt we got on so well. And I think when people who share the same energy let their fires burn even brighter, there are no limits! Did you feel the same when we met? I'm actually married, but it doesn't matter because chance encounters are always the result of destiny. Next time we meet, I want to forget about the time and talk with you till morning. It would be amazing to get to know you better. But it's up to you whether you're ready for that. It would be a shame if you weren't brave enough to go for it, but if you aren't, you don't need to reply! I'll take it like a man.'

For some reason, I was suddenly being forced into a choice between taking things in a new direction (it was probably fair to interpret this as meaning a romantic relationship) or stopping communication altogether.

While I was still digesting this, mouth agape, a message popped up from Tsuchiya, my first match. There was something off-key about this one, too.

'So *Sex in Japan* is a novel then? Very interesting, thank you for recommending it to me. It's about swinging, is that something you're interested in? Did the book change your perspective on sex? As a man, I often wonder if women get excited about being looked at and desired, because they're on the receiving end after all. I'd love to talk about the book with you next time we meet. I know a great barbecue restaurant in Meguro – how about sometime next week?'

Okay, okay, I thought. *So this is how it is, is it? Right. I see.*

It seemed that even with my looks and my age (thirty-three and married – though currently separated; no children) I still had it. What these two messages told me was that in these circles (or whatever you called them), there was still demand for someone like me. To be honest, it was a relief: it was like going for a medical check-up and being told everything is fine.

But this relief was far from the excitement I'd felt when I'd met these two men. Both times we'd been able to develop a rapport and enjoy the conversation, and I'd felt as though something was beginning, as though I'd taken the plunge into something new. And I'd thought so hard about the books, too, and picked the best I could, recommending them in the hope that my matches really would be interested. But in the end, for both these men, the possibility of sex with a woman had taken on a life of its own and overshadowed that.

A frustrating feeling of powerlessness settled over me like a black cloud.

And yet – I wanted to keep going just a little longer.

*

TOKYO IS AN OPEN DOOR

My third match was called Harada. I wondered if my mistake had been having the two previous meetings in the evening, so I tried arranging this one for the middle of the day, on one of my days off. Several people responded to my listing this time, so I picked the one who seemed the most respectable. Being able to choose meant I could avoid anyone I couldn't find out anything about, which was a bit of a relief.

I arrived at the appointed Starbucks to find the man I presumed to be Harada already sitting at a table. He was slim and wore a turtleneck. On the table next to his coffee was a pack of playing cards. Unlike my first two matches, who'd come in all guns blazing, Harada seemed urbane and composed. We'd only just finished saying hello when he took the lead by proposing he perform some magic for me.

'Oh, okay,' I said.

That was right: Harada's profile had said, 'I'll show you some magic tricks. I'm also interested in photography and writing poetry, and I update my blog daily.'

I was a little surprised at the abrupt suggestion, but the magic tricks were actually very entertaining and well worth watching. Harada also seemed more confident and happier when he was showing me the tricks than during the initial small talk.

He performed trick after trick, like a salesman demoing kitchen appliances. After about fifteen minutes, when half our allotted time was up, he said, 'Well, that's about it,' gathered together the cards and put them back in their case. Next, he took out a black folder.

'I also do photography and poetry,' he said. 'Would you like to have a look? Let me know if you have any thoughts on any of it.'

'Oh, okay. Of course.'

I tentatively opened the folder and found a romantic photo of a mass of cosmos flowers, with a Ferris wheel gleaming in the background. On top of the photo was printed a poem in an elegant serif typeface. The poetry gave Harada another dimension, quite removed from the impression he made at first glance, and different again from his magic tricks.

Memory
I wonder: What is parting for?
Since losing you, I've thought of little else
I look at the sky and see your smile
But I can't yet bring myself to smile like you,
   laughing up at the blue
Once more, the seasons come around
And I wonder: How are you?

The photos were of the city at night, flowers, the sky, sunsets, fallen leaves in pools of water, cups of coffee and four-leaved clovers. A lot of the poems were about love or had romantic messages ('Eventually this downpour, too, will cease / And the rainbow stretching across the sky will be all the more beautiful').

For a while, I found myself sunk in silence.

'Do you . . . take your photos with a digital camera? They're really lovely . . .' I said. It wasn't a very imaginative question, but I wanted to fill the gaping silence and it was the first thing I could think of. We continued in this vein, me looking through the folder and asking uninspiring questions, like 'Why do you write poems?' and 'When do you write poems?' and 'Are you writing about yourself?' and Harada giving almost monosyllabic answers.

'Are there any you particularly like?' he asked.

'Oh, well . . . that first one, of the Ferris wheel, that's really beautiful.'

'Ah, a lot of people choose that one.'

'And then this one, maybe, and this one . . .' I showed him the ones I meant, and felt relieved when he seemed faintly pleased. By now we were passing the thirty-minute mark, so I hastily moved on.

'Oh yes, that reminds me – what I do is make book recommendations. I haven't really asked you much about yourself . . . But is there anything in particular you like reading?'

'Hmm, let me think . . . I don't actually read books that often. Or poetry, either – I'm self-taught, I suppose you could say; I really just write whatever comes into my head. I'd like to read a poetry collection, anything really, if you can recommend one,' he said. I already had an idea, so this time I decided to recommend the book there and then.

'Okay. Have you heard of a poet called Noriko Ibaragi?' I asked.

'No, I don't think I have.'

'Well, you could read any of her collections, but if you were going to read just one, I'd recommend *Women's Words*. It's a sort of best-of. I know Shuntaro Tanikawa is probably the most famous Japanese poet, but Noriko Ibaragi's poems have a stronger message and they really touch your heart – maybe some of the expressions she uses will give you inspiration for your own poetry. She combines purity with boldness, and puts them into words so succinctly, but with such feeling. I find her poems so moving, I really love them.'

'That's very interesting. I'd like to read them too, then,' said Harada. And just like that, we parted. It was so easy, I was almost disappointed. Compared to the dogged enthusiasm of my previous two matches, today's excess of cool was refreshing. I'd assumed that with PerfectStrangers, the idea was to try to get to know all about one another, but now I saw you could just spend your thirty minutes showing someone whatever it was you wanted to show them. You were free to do what you liked . . .

It felt like a new door had opened.

*

My fourth match was a man called Ohashi. He was in his mid-twenties or thereabouts, and his appearance was oddly incongruous: he wore a smart suit he didn't seem comfortable in, paired with a glaring bright blue rucksack, like a schoolboy who'd just joined the workforce.

It was a Friday night, and the Doutor coffee shop in Shibuya looked crowded. Ohashi was waiting outside and when he caught sight of me, he greeted me with a nod of the head and a natural smile.

'It looks busy in there. Shall we try somewhere a bit quieter?' I said.

'No, it's okay, it'll probably quieten down soon,' he said, and then he turned and dived straight in, ordered a drink for himself, told me he'd go and find a table, then briskly headed off up the stairs. I hastily ordered myself an iced tea and followed him.

We eventually managed to find seats at a table for two. Once we'd introduced ourselves and had a chance to draw breath, Ohashi said, 'I'm studying mentalism at the moment. I'll show you, if you like.' He took a ten-yen coin from his wallet and handed it to me. 'Hold this in one hand, but don't let me see which one. Then put both fists out in front of you and I'll guess which hand it's in.'

Mentalism? Is that a thing people do now? I thought it was just that DaiGo guy off the TV. But I didn't say anything. Instead, I clasped the coin in one hand and put both fists on the table as instructed.

'Now, this isn't the same as just guessing by intuition,' he said. 'It's about judging by observing those tiny flickers of expression you make when I ask you which hand it's in. Yes – so don't open your hand until I ask you to, please. And don't tell me whether I'm right or wrong yet. Hmm . . . Could it be the right, perhaps . . . ?'

He surveyed my face meaningfully. I tried to keep my expression blank, but distracting thoughts came creeping in. *He's so sure of himself, it's going to be really awkward if he gets it wrong. Please get it right, please get it right . . .*

'Okay, got it. It's in your left hand, isn't it? Open up, please,' he said.

With a sinking feeling, I opened my empty left hand.

'What . . .?' he said. He seemed genuinely flustered, and I couldn't help feeling sorry for him.

'But it's because I was trying really hard to convince you it was in that one!' I said, desperately massaging his ego. 'I guess I win this round! It was tense, though, I thought you were going to see right through me. You've got great powers of observation!'

'Oh right, I see. You got me! You must be an actress or something. Like Sayuri Yoshinaga – I mean, even DaiGo couldn't read her when he tried mentalism on her recently,' he said, sharing with me this nugget of information from the world of TV, which was presumably where he had picked up this stuff.

Still – he was a good person not to show any bad feeling or resentment when he'd failed, even after launching in with such confidence.

'I'm not learning mentalism so I can abuse it, or anything – I'm going to use it to communicate better with people,' Ohashi told me.

On the basis of this, I recommended him *The Art of Funny*, a humorous parody of a business book that explains techniques for making your conversation partner laugh. It's not just an amusing read, though; it actually touches on some truths about communication that really make you sit up and think. How important it is to work out what kind of humour will go down well during a conversation, for example, and how to fine tune your approach to make a good impression.

'Oh, that sounds great! It might help with my studies, too,' Ohashi said delightedly.

'Are you a psychologist or a counsellor or something?' I asked, not out of any particular interest, but more to fill a gap in the conversation.

Ohashi said he wasn't, then he hummed and hawed evasively for a while. Then, as though talking half to himself, he said, 'Actually, I'm being headhunted by that big ad agency Hakuhodo at the moment, it's a bit of a pain. But I'm already on fifty million yen a year, so . . . Oh, sorry – shouldn't have said that!'

Well. That was some piece of unsolicited information he'd thoughtfully furnished me with. Fifty million yen – that had to be, what, ten times the average salary? I *wanted* to be impressed, I really did. 'What? Fifty million yen a year?' I wanted to say. 'That's crazy! You earn that much, and you still come to a place like Doutor and split the bill? Well I never.'

But I just couldn't bring myself to say it. If only he'd said ten million yen, I'd have still been surprised, but I think I could have believed it. But fifty million? What was I supposed to say to that? Or was he making up this obviously ridiculous figure as some kind of joke? It didn't seem as though he was expecting me to laugh . . .

I thought and thought, but only got more tied up in knots. By now I'd left an uncomfortably long silence, so I just said, 'Mm . . .?' and took a sip of my iced tea.

'Oh, it looks like time's nearly up. Shall we head out?' he said.

'Ah, so it is. Yes, okay.'

We cleared away our glasses and trays and left Doutor.

So. I'd met a man who tried his luck by bringing up sex. A man who told me he was married, but it was no big deal. A man who spent lots of time showing me his magic tricks and poems. And a man who told a bizarre lie about earning fifty million yen a year. Was everyone on the site like this? Wasn't it just a bit too much?

Yes – ridiculous, I thought. And yet, as I walked towards Shibuya Station with Mr Fifty Million, the throng of people around me seemed more colourful, more vibrant than usual.

Until now, this city had only ever felt cold and inhospitable to me. But what a mad, interesting place it had turned out to be when I'd just tried opening a door! What freedom there was here! You could do whatever you liked – *I* could do whatever I liked. If I wanted to introduce books to people, then that was what I was going to do.

As we waited for the lights at Shibuya Crossing, I burned with this newfound enthusiasm. Beside me, Mr Fifty Million said, 'Um . . .' as though broaching a tricky subject. 'By the way, Nanako . . . You know your profile is quite weird, don't you? I think you should probably change it. I like a challenge, so I wanted to meet you today to find out what you were like. And

I was relieved because you're actually quite normal. But a lot of people might think you're a bit weird. If you do your profile properly, you'll be able to meet a lot more decent people.'

Excuse me . . . ?

Well, *that* I did not expect. I had been so busy harbouring my own suspicions about potential matches, I had never considered the possibility that they might be suspicious of *me*.

I'd thought that on a site like PerfectStrangers, the important thing was to stand out and not get lost in the crowd, so I'd written my profile in a way I imagined would go down well. I'd put down my occupation as 'sexy bookseller', and what was more, when I listed the chat Ohashi had responded to, I'd even posed a risqué riddle, of all things: 'What gets harder the hotter things get? If you know the answer, I'd love to meet you!' (The answer was 'Staying hydrated' . . .) And then for my profile picture . . . for my profile picture I'd used a selfie of me, poker-faced, wearing a cuddly toy on my head. A right Little Miss Quirky.

The toy was a *tsuchinoko*, a chubby snake-like creature brought back from the future in an episode of *Doraemon*. This particular piece of merchandise was actually meant to be used as a tissue-box cover. But at home I'd got into the habit of wearing it as a hat, and at some point I'd thought, *You know what? This looks really cute!* and had taken a selfie with it on, hence the photo.

The more I thought about it, the more dejected I felt. I was in no position to laugh at a would-be DaiGo who got flustered when he struggled to guess which hand the coin was in. I looked questionable enough myself. Like an absolute weirdo, in fact. I'd had no right to get up on my high horse and think *All right, I'll go along with your game* – because it turned out *I* was the dodgy-looking one. And it was doubly excruciating because it had taken another dodgy character to point it out to me.

I wanted to curl up and die.

'You're right . . . You're totally right. I've just realised how weird it looks. I'll change it straight away,' I said.

'I think that's definitely a good idea!' said Ohashi.

Thank you, Mr Fifty Million, I thought. *I'll believe in your salary, if only for tonight.*

The lights went green. We waved goodbye, and I left that mad city behind.

*

While Ohashi was the first to point out the issues with my profile, its quality and my chat listings were dramatically improved still further thanks to Ida, my very next match.

Big and burly like the baseball player Hideki Matsui, Ida was a cheerful insurance salesman with a friendly conversational manner. He said he'd set himself up in business as a freelancer. Maybe it was his profession that gave him such a reassuring presence: he was courteous like a salesperson, but easy to talk to.

'You're not a sexy bookseller anymore, then? I saw it's gone from your profile,' he said.

'Don't remind me, please . . .' I said. I'd written the description myself, but hearing someone say it out loud made me want to crawl into a hole.

'Hah! Don't worry. I was just messaging a friend from PerfectStrangers and we were saying it looked like someone interesting had joined up. So you meet people and recommend books to them, then?'

'Yes. To be honest, I thought if I stood out on the site a bit more I'd get more likes and move up the popularity rankings, so I wrote those weird things to try and give my profile a bit of oomph. But the last person I met told me if people think you're odd, they're less likely to meet you. So I've just deleted that stuff.'

'Ah, I see. Who was it you met last? Ohashi? Hmm . . . so he's actually all right, then,' Ida muttered, and I realised he must have met Ohashi too. That 'actually' didn't slip by me, either – it sounded as though Ida hadn't thought much of him. I wanted to ask if it was because of the salary thing – had he told Ida fifty million too? – but I thought better of it.

'So you've got the details of ten thousand books? That's pretty amazing,' Ida said with an easy smile.

'Well, I haven't actually read them all,' I replied. 'But we were reorganising at the shop I manage and I got to look at the list of all the books we'd stocked in the past year, and I saw there were about thirteen thousand. I order them all in myself, and I can pretty much remember the covers and what kind of books they are, so I thought I'd go with that.'

'I see. Actually, I think recommending books is a great idea. You'll definitely get more interest on the site by being clearer about what you want to do, instead of trying to make yourself look eccentric. And you'll get to meet people who are keen to see what you're doing as well. Have you recommended books to the people you've met so far?'

'Yes. I gave some of them my recommendation in person, and for others I thought about it for a bit and then sent it via Messenger a few days later.'

Ida put his hand to his chin as though pondering what I'd told him. He nodded to himself, and then said, 'Why not give the people you met a quick heads-up and then post your book recommendations below their profiles? There's a comments section there where you can leave reviews for users after you've met them. That way, other users will be able to browse your profile and see you recommending books – it'll be good publicity for you. And people who haven't seen your profile will come across your comments on other people's profiles, and it might get them interested too.'

'Oh, I get it . . . I hadn't thought that far ahead.'

'And don't just write about it in your profile – mention it when you list a chat, too, so people who look at the listing can see it straight away. At the moment, someone has to be looking at your profile specifically, and then they have to click the "Read more" button before they get to your comment about books, so there's a chance people won't see it.'

'Yes, you're right . . . !' I said.

'Would you mind just logging in for a minute?' Ida asked. He opened up the PerfectStrangers homepage on his laptop and passed it over to me to enter my details. I logged in and passed the laptop back to him. With practised hands, and without hesitation, he began to deftly edit my profile.

'First, try putting this here . . . then deleting this . . .'

In the blink of an eye, my profile was looking so polished that I thought, *Yes, I'd ask her for a book recommendation – even if I say so myself.* Disappointingly, the one thing Ida couldn't change was the photo of me being Little Miss Quirky with the cuddly toy on my head. But never mind – I could take a better photo later.

'That's wonderful! Thank you so much!' I said.

'No problem at all. I just hope this means you can keep getting the most out of PerfectStrangers. I really want you to like the site, and enjoy using it,' said Ida, sounding every bit as though he was on the sales team or something.

'Why would you go to all that trouble for me? Is it just because you like the site?' I asked.

'I know it seems strange, but I've been a member of PerfectStrangers since it started, I guess. I've been using it since the early days. I really like how the site works and I've made loads of good friends through it – so I want to look after it.

'You can have really interesting encounters with people on PerfectStrangers, but it's always being infiltrated by people doing multi-level marketing and pyramid selling and things. People trying to get you to sign up to weird religious groups, things like that. So there are a few of us who call ourselves the Perfect-Strangers Police, and if we find anyone who looks potentially dodgy, we try to meet them in person, kind of pretending we might be interested, and we get them to talk about it and then make them quit the site.'

Yes, that was right – soliciting people to join pyramid schemes and religious groups was explicitly forbidden on PerfectStrangers. If you were found doing it, you'd be banned.

'I mean, I'm a freelance insurance salesman, but I don't recommend insurance products to people I've met on Perfect-Strangers, unless someone particularly asks me to,' Ida said.

After that, he gave me some recommendations for people to meet, and told me I should try and chat with them if I could find times that worked.

Up until now, I'd thought meeting people through PerfectStrangers was like going head to head in one-to-one combat with one person from among the countless many, and then doing it all over again with someone else. So it was interesting that, beneath the surface, PerfectStrangers was actually more like one big community – like a village, even, where the members gradually got to know one another and deepen their relationships and trust. And it seemed to me that it must be a good community, if people were taking such care to protect it.

'When the site first started, there were loads of really interesting people around and it was great fun. Now people are more normal, it's got a bit ordinary – a bit dull, maybe. So I'm genuinely happy you've joined. I'm expecting great things!' Ida said. He reminded me of a high-school pupil in his final year, bemoaning the new clutch of first years for being too meek. Was this him acknowledging me as one to watch?

More to the point, when I'd first come up with the idea of recommending a book to each person, I'd thought, *This is going to be so cool!* But the reactions from my first few matches didn't seem to mirror my enthusiasm, and I'd been on the verge of losing confidence, thinking that it wasn't going down very well, and that maybe people didn't really read that much after all. So I was happy someone was praising my idea at last, and I felt motivated. If I was going to get to meet more people like Ida, then I would keep trying.

For the rest of our chat, we talked enthusiastically about Kyoto. We both loved the city. I'd lived there for about a year and a half in my late twenties when I'd been relocated there for work, and I'd been constantly dashing all over the place, guidebook in hand, to make the most of my limited time there. Ida, meanwhile, had fallen under Kyoto's spell recently, and he said he went there at weekends – or even there and back in a day sometimes. We were alike in that it wasn't the city's many shrines and temples we felt drawn to, so much as the city streets themselves, and the local culture.

'In that case, Ida, do you know *Meets* magazine?' I asked.

'Yeah, of course! The local magazine about the Kansai area? I really like it! It's great, they've got really deep insider knowledge.'

'Yeah, and their guide to Kyoto is totally different from other guide books, it's very cool. Actually, *Meets* used to be even cooler, if that's possible. It was started by this guy called Hiroki Ko – he's written a book about how he started the magazine, and the book is really excellent, too. His philosophy was totally different from what you get with other local magazines and guide books – he talks about the process of finding the voice of a city and setting it down on paper. And I feel like you and Ko are kind of awesome in the same way. I definitely think you'd like the book!'

'Aw, that's really nice of you! It sounds great, what's it called? I'd love to give it a read.'

'It's *The Road to Meets: The Age of the Neighbourhood Magazine.*'

I'd been a huge fan of *Meets* from the magazine's early days, and Ko's book was something I really treasured, but until now I'd never found anyone I wanted to share it with. So I was delighted I'd been able to introduce the book to Ida, and in the course of what had been such a pleasant conversation. I'd just naturally found myself thinking I'd really love him to read it, and I felt a surge of joy that the recommendation had come about in such a nice way.

Yes, this is it, I thought. *This is what I love.*

CHAPTER 2

I LOVE YOU, VILLAGE VANGUARD

I had embarked on a sort-of experiment I didn't really understand with a sort-of dating site I didn't really understand, and one of my reasons for doing so was Yoshida, my boss at Village Vanguard. Not so long before I'd walked out of the apartment and not returned, I had unexpectedly found myself in the back room of the shop presenting to Yoshida the merits of thirty different books.

*

It was now more than ten years since I'd joined Village Vanguard. My first encounter with the shop had been another five years before that, around the time I started university. It was the Village Vanguard in Tokyo's trendy Shimokitazawa neighbourhood. I'd gone along there with a friend, who'd said they had a cool place to show me.

The shop's roomy interior was packed with a jumble of miscellaneous books, manga comics, CDs and novelty goods, and all sorts of items were hanging from the ceiling. The aisles were narrow and dimly lit, and it was like walking through the jungle, or a haunted house. All the random assorted items on display were grotesque or surreal, and the cloth screens stuck over the windows to keep out the sunlight were patterned with skulls and marijuana and psychedelia, the gaps in between messily plugged with posters of Bob Marley or *Trainspotting*. And the counter, the walls, the floor – every available surface – was plastered with handwritten signs, pieces of yellow paper like oversized Post-it notes, scrawled on in black marker pen – POP signs, they were called. Each bore a comment about the product to which it was affixed – but they were all jokey, as though whoever had written them wasn't that bothered about selling the items. I found myself excited by the chaos of the space.

I didn't get on very well with my parents and I had never really settled in at school. Aside from my few friends, it was only my books and niche interests that provided me with solace. In middle school I'd discovered the work of manga artist Kyoko Okazaki and Shibuya-kei pop music, and since then I'd been completely devoted to all things alternative. So for me, Village Vanguard was a place filled with meaning and wonder, a treasure trove of all the things I loved best.

Displayed alongside the manga by my beloved Kyoko Okazaki were almost all the women's comics I was interested in by Kiriko Nananan, Q-ta Minami, Naito Yamada . . . In the men's manga section they had the books by Taiyo Matsumoto that I had been coveting, as well as Santa Inoue, Katsuhiro Otomo and many others. The novels section featured the authors I liked, but also piles of books I'd never even heard of before, and plenty that looked interesting. Until then I'd only thought of books as novels, paperbacks; I'd hardly ever seen books on subjects like architecture and art. But here, books in every genre you could imagine were arranged side by side and given equal importance.

I want to discover everything they have in here, I thought.

From that day onwards, I frequented that shop like it was an addiction. After graduating from university, my obsession finally came to a head and I moved to Shimokitazawa. When I thought about how I'd be able to visit Village Vanguard every day, I couldn't stop smiling. I hadn't had much luck with job hunting, and I already worked part-time in the nightlife industry and wasn't struggling to make ends meet, so I decided that for now, I would just take it easy and enjoy myself until I was thirty. So there I was, a typical aimless young person living the Shimokita life.

And then one day, I was paying my usual visit to the shop when my eye was caught by a piece of paper stuck up on the door: NEW SHOP OPENING IN ROPPONGI HILLS! LOTS OF STAFF WANTED.

Well, if I was just taking it easy for now, wouldn't it make sense to work at Village Vanguard? So I applied, they accepted – and that was how I joined the company.

I thoroughly enjoyed getting to spend from morning until evening each day with the new shop's manager and the other staff my age. I had been socially useless at school and university, and in any sort of communal activity I'd tried – but now I surprised myself with how much I looked forward to my part-time gig every day. Back then, staff were free to have dyed hair, tattoos, facial piercings – you name it – and the whole company had a friendly, inclusive ethos, accepting social dropouts with no judgement. There were so many eccentric characters around, so much individuality, that the word 'individuality' didn't really mean anything anymore. This was the environment in which I found myself, and I felt more at home than I had expected.

When I first started working at Village Vanguard, I had the mindset that I was just there to enjoy myself. I was simply having fun being on the till with my fellow part-timers. But little by little, I began to feel that I wanted to try making it my Real Job. The shop had only just opened and a lot of staff had joined at the same time, so there was a sense of competition among us. We were all free to write whatever we wanted on the yellow POP signs, and I was delighted if I wrote a sign for a product and the product sold well; I'd get enthused and start thinking about what clever thing I could write on the next one. The staff in each branch of Village Vanguard had full control over the running of their shop, and even as a part-timer only three months into the job, I was in charge of ordering in our stock, so I had plenty of opportunity to experience the joys of luring in customers and enticing them to buy.

However, the bar job I'd taken out of curiosity before joining Village Vanguard was also starting to get interesting. This was another establishment with a strong alternative flavour; it had a real gothic aesthetic and was frequented by male cross-dressers and those with an S&M persuasion. I was no good at working the room and keeping a whole crowd of customers entertained, but there were some slightly gloomier characters who tended to show up on their own, and those people I found I could comfortably talk to at length.

While I was working, I would be thinking about what I personally could give back to the customers who'd been good enough to visit us. And when I adopted that mindset, for the first time ever I really got the sense that my job was worthwhile. I could actually see my efforts bearing fruit: customers asked for me by name, and the number of regulars increased. It felt like my existence was being acknowledged and it made me happy.

But when the time finally came to pick just one job, I chose Village Vanguard. Back then they'd never had a female shop manager, so that became my new goal.

Once I'd made it to manager, I enjoyed setting up my shop how I liked and achieving good sales figures. But almost without noticing, I found my interest was leaning away from the novelty items and towards the books. When I first joined the company, I'd been very keen on their stock of niche-interest goods and the general atmosphere of the place, but once I was actually working there, I started to discover other new things to enjoy.

Let's try displaying that book next to this one, I would think, and *Why not shelve that book in this genre instead?* and *If I stick this POP sign on that book, people might stop and take a look at it.* I built up a huge repertoire of books that I really wanted customers to buy – I was sure they'd fly off the shelves once people knew more about them – and I took particular pleasure in trying to sell those books using the power of my own words.

My sales technique wasn't reserved for works of literature I had a particular attachment to. It could also be applied to books that, on first glance, would seem to resist comment: books of landscape photos, for example, or practical volumes like cookbooks. I would stare at the covers and ask myself, *What words can I use to really highlight the appeal of this book?* I found I was becoming able to discern what was special about books that perhaps didn't look so promising at first, and to distil their charm into words.

People at the company started to notice the way I sold the books and wrote the POP signs, and for a while they made a great fuss of me. I was put in charge of the books in the Shimokitazawa shop, something I had always declared to the company as being my ultimate goal, and I also got to order in new product ranges and pick the books for new shops.

But times changed, huge branches of the shop were opened in out-of-town shopping centres, and the direction of the company gradually shifted. They began to focus less on the books and more on the novelty goods, which were easier to sell and had better profit margins. In the past, the things we sold had always been of questionable use. A lot of it was junk, in the best possible way: silly knick-knacks. But at some point we'd found that, if we didn't keep buying in the latest merchandise featuring popular mascots and manga and anime characters, we could no longer keep up our sales.

A lot of employees were concerned at the way Village Vanguard's cultural standing was falling, and I felt a sense of personal crisis at how the company was changing. So I appealed directly to the head of the company and said that, with the book section being scaled down the way it was, we were going to lose our customer appeal. I built up a network of publishers and distributors, and gathered together like-minded colleagues to organise our own Village Vanguard-style book fairs in store. I tried new idea after new idea. But the decline continued and, along with many of the more conservative long-time staff members, I came to feel as though I'd lost the place where I belonged. At one point, I looked around and realised that almost all the staff members who'd been there before me, and who I'd admired so much, had left.

And yet the fact remained that Village Vanguard was where I'd learned the joy of work, and the joy of bookselling. I didn't think I would ever stop loving the place. Besides, I'd dedicated most of my life to the company, and I no longer knew how to walk away.

*

I met Yoshida not long after I started at Village Vanguard. That was ten years ago, when he managed the Roppongi Hills shop and I was a part-timer there.

The first time we talked about books, we were taking a break in the back room. Out of the blue, Yoshida said, 'Have you come across Hiroshi Homura? Really interesting,' and fished a book out of his bag to show me. It was a recently published collection of essays entitled *Time You Went Home*. I had never heard of Homura before, but Yoshida's endorsement was enough to make me think there must be something special about the book. I began reading it for myself and was instantly hooked; I'd genuinely never read anything so fascinating before. Yoshida was delighted when I told him this, and after that the two of us began to talk books together.

In the end, the Roppongi Hills shop was closed down after only a year. All of us – the employees who'd been part of the company before, and the new part-timers who wanted to stay on – were relocated to branches throughout Japan and ended up in different places, but I kept in touch with Yoshida now and again.

'Hey Nana-chan, have you read Mimi Hachikai?'

'Hi Yoshida, Shinsuke Yoshitake's just published a collection of sketches!'

'I just read a book by Shiro Maeda for the first time, I really liked it.'

'Speaking of playwrights – Sohei Wakusaka's book about schoolchildren is interesting too.'

We had plenty of brief, sporadic exchanges, recommending each other books whenever they came into our heads. Yoshida gradually came to feel less like a boss and more like a friend.

He was good-looking and seemed like the perfect package as long as he didn't open his mouth. He was always calm and collected at work: unflappable, and a quick thinker. Other people put a lot of trust in him, and I respected the way he did his job, but there were some things about him that meant he never quite attained coolness in my eyes.

For example, if a normal person tripped over, they'd probably laugh it off and look sheepish. If it happened to Yoshida, he would just carry on walking, completely expressionless, as though nothing had happened. Having witnessed the whole thing, I'd say to him, half-teasing: 'Um, hang on. You *did* just trip over, didn't you?' But he would maintain a poker face and insist that he hadn't.

When we went out with colleagues after work, Yoshida would sit there quietly, coolly sipping his drink, while beside him an excitable employee would say something that made everyone laugh. While the chatter moved on and everyone's attention was elsewhere, in a quiet voice Yoshida would repeat word for word whatever funny thing had just been said, in whispered mimicry.

Everyone had this image of Yoshida as being very cool and capable, and no one else had discovered his quirks. I alone continued to observe in secret the other interesting side to him – the part that was a little offbeat, like Hiroshi Homura.

*

It was ten years since we'd become acquainted as shop manager and part-timer, and Yoshida was now the Kanto regional manager. He periodically came to inspect my shop and knew I was becoming disillusioned. During one particular inspection, after he'd checked that sales were improving, he looked at the huge display of commercial character-themed merchandise at the shop's entrance and said, 'I can see you're doing your best to put up with it,' with a dry laugh. Then as he was leaving he said, 'Why don't you think of some books to recommend to me next time I'm here?'

I was no longer enjoying work at all. I was unhappy with the company because they weren't putting any effort into selling books anymore, a fact I'd been loudly bemoaning – but even in my own shop, I was run off my feet all day trying to deal with the novelty goods and I never managed to get round to the book section myself. It had become a wasteland, devoid of any titles I actually wanted to recommend. I took Yoshida's suggestion as his roundabout way of pointing this out and trying to get me to do something about it.

What was more, I knew I would normally have been transferred to a branch in a smaller town at this point in my career, but Yoshida had deftly arranged for me to be in Yokohama where he could keep an eye on me and look after me. I knew, too, that he had caught several mistakes I'd made at work and dealt with them for me. He was doing a lot on my behalf.

I was mortified.

So the next time he came, I planned to be prepared. In fact, I'd be *over* prepared, so much so that he'd laugh and say, 'You didn't have to go that far!' That was my aim, at least – but it would be difficult to whip the book section into shape in just a month or so. What could I do?

Then I had an idea: what if I tried filling a whole box with books to recommend to him? It wouldn't have much to do with the shop itself anymore, but maybe that was fine. It struck me that Yoshida and I hadn't been talking about books at all recently. So I settled on this plan, and decided to list everything I could think of about Yoshida from our ten years of acquaintance, and then choose some books based on that list. I made notes about the books he'd read, his favourite authors, his personality, the things he'd said, the things we'd talked about . . .

I remembered I'd read Keiichiro Hirano's *What Am I?* recently and I was sure Yoshida would like it. He really enjoyed discussing books that dealt with the idea of self-awareness. Oh yes – and along those lines, had he read the manga *Wild Mountain* by Hideyasu Moto? There had been some time before the final instalment of the series was published and I'd only just got to the end myself, but it was the kind of thing you had to read all the way through. If Yoshida hadn't read it yet, I'd have to recommend it. And maybe he hadn't come across *Poten Life*, either? That was definitely the sort of thing he'd enjoy. There was Yu Nagashima, of course, but Yoshida would probably already be familiar with his work. And going off on a completely different tangent, had he read *Cities, Consumption and the*

Disney Dream? After all, on his last visit we'd talked about what was going to happen to all those big shopping centres. I'd found the book pretty interesting . . .

Once I started thinking about it, any number of titles sprang to mind, but I found myself stalling at around ten definites. Ten books slightly lacked impact, though . . . I would keep thinking until I had another twenty or so, even if it took all day. With my notes in hand, I set out for a bookshop in the city centre to search for more contenders.

I wanted each book to be included for a reason: because it suited some facet of Yoshida's personality, or because it picked up on something he'd talked about. I piled volume after volume into a cardboard box in preparation for the big event. When Yoshida got in touch to say he'd be in the next day, there were thirty books in there. I looked at each one and thought about how I would present it and what I would say, and I kept changing the order – shuffling and reshuffling, taking books out of the box and putting them back in, taking them out and putting them back in, over and over again.

And now here we were in the shop's back room, among the piles of novelty items that hadn't sold. I sat opposite Yoshida and took out the book on the very top.

'Okay, here's the first one I want to introduce to you!' I said, and began my presentation. It had started as a bit of fun, but now, for some reason, I was incredibly nervous. At some point I had begun taking it very seriously.

I must have been on the receiving end of people selling books and novelties hundreds of times before, but I'd never realised that selling things to someone face to face like this could bring you out in such an unpleasant sweat. As I talked, Yoshida said, 'Uh-huh?' and 'I see, I see,' and he took the books as I finished with them and began to arrange them in two piles, one on his left and one on his right.

'Um . . . which pile is which?' I asked.

'Don't worry about it, I'll tell you afterwards. Just keep going.'

Now I had become inordinately conscious of where he was looking, and of any slight movement or gesture he made.

Is he interested? Am I boring him, is he just pretending to listen?

I tried to read his expression, but I couldn't really tell what he was thinking. I wondered whether thirty books was too many, after all. I was sure he must be getting bored. Part way through, I began to present the books more briefly. There were a few jokey ones that were just in there for laughs, and as I introduced them I tried to gauge his reaction and the general feeling; sometimes I would say, 'I was going to tell you about this one, but actually, maybe it's not quite right . . . Let's leave it.'

And then, finally, the box was empty. I had talked far too much and worried far too much, and I was exhausted.

Yoshida split the two piles up into smaller piles and swapped various books around, and then he held out seven of them and said, 'Okay, I'll take these.' Maybe he was just taking pity on me as my boss. Maybe he was making himself buy the books even though he hadn't been interested in any of them. Still – I took the seven volumes from him, feeling so happy I could cry.

I had never thought so seriously before about which books to recommend to someone. After all, you could suggest a book to someone without even considering what kind of person they were, and without having any particular reason. The strongest and simplest endorsement for a book was that you yourself had read it and enjoyed it. Magazines and newspapers featured lists of books, and books were lined up for sale in shops; surely these were ways of recommending books without pinpointing a specific reader?

No, I thought. *It's just not the same.*

Because you couldn't recommend a book to someone if you didn't know them, not really. And you couldn't recommend a book if you didn't know it well yourself. And moreover, you couldn't recommend a book without a good reason. You had to *want* that person to read it, because you'd thought about what that specific book would mean to them.

I didn't really know what it was I'd experienced, what it was that had just revealed itself to me for the first time. I'd really enjoyed digging deep into Yoshida as a person and thinking of books for him – but had he got anything out of it? Was he pleased?

I wasn't sure. And yet the echoes of that excitement stubbornly lingered on in my mind. I wanted to get to know the feeling better.

*

When I'd first come across PerfectStrangers and had racked my brains for a way to use the site, for some reason it was this episode with Yoshida that had sprung to mind. I wanted to try recommending books to people again. I realised, of course, that it would be more difficult choosing books for people I didn't know. But the buzz I'd experienced that first time was propelling me forwards, driving me onwards – even in the direction of complete strangers.

CHAPTER 3

LIFE STARTS TO MOVE

My journey had got off to a shaky, unpredictable start, but I was gradually beginning to find my feet. And what an engrossing journey it was turning out to be. I felt like a child, staring in awe at some wondrous country that I was seeing for the very first time. I hadn't yet got a real sense of how well my book recommendations were being received, but nevertheless, after every meeting I would go home and call to mind the person I had met, agonise over this book and that until I'd eventually narrowed it down to one, and then write my match a message. It was a task I took a lot of pleasure in.

That is, until I met Takashima.

Takashima was the quintessential digital nomad, something that was very in vogue at the time. When I met him, he was travelling the country with his MacBook, frequenting local Starbucks cafés where he would work at his tech job. It was my first time talking to someone living that lifestyle, and I couldn't help bombarding him with questions. We chatted away in good spirits and had a thoroughly agreeable time together.

Digital nomad that he was, Takashima was interested in the future of work, and in new lifestyles for a new era. As soon as I got home, I promptly messaged him with a few books I'd thought of. There was Raymond Mungo's *Cosmic Profit: How to Make Money Without Doing Time*, and Yoshiaki Nishimura's *Make Your Work!* – basically bibles for new working styles. Then there were a few titles that had had a lot of press recently: Kyohei Sakaguchi's *Build Your Own Independent Nation*; Hayato Ikeda's *Living Freely on 1.5 Million Yen a Year*; and Noritoshi Furuichi's *The Happy Youth of a Desperate Country*.

They were all books I'd read recently and really enjoyed, and each had given me plenty of food for thought, so I suggested them to Takashima with excitement, sure they'd be useful to him at this stage in his life. But—

'I read all those ages ago,' was his brief reply.

His message poured cold water over my erstwhile elation. But it also helped open my eyes.

If I'd given it even a little thought, it should have been obvious. He was an expert in digital nomadism, I suppose you could say, whereas I was just a dabbler, my nomad knowledge only superficial. How could I possibly pick a book that would surprise him? I felt the beginnings of a slight resentment. If he'd already read a load of books, I wished he'd told me earlier . . . But no, it was on me. I hadn't questioned him thoroughly enough.

I regretted not talking about books with him a little more during our meeting, not sounding him out more. Anyway, time for a rethink. Perhaps, instead of books on specific social theories and ways of working, it would be better to pick something more universal, something that encompassed more abstract themes. Would an adventure novel suit him? I added two more recommendations: Jon Krakauer's *Into the Wild* and Richard Bach's *Illusions*. But then came the swift reply – 'I've read those too' – and I despaired. Was he just going to say the same thing, no matter what I suggested . . . ?

I had a good think before I played my next card: a book called *The Children's Story*. It's an allegory casting a shadow of doubt over dictatorships, set in a primary-school classroom with an atmosphere so tense you could cut it with a knife. One morning, the children suddenly find they have a new teacher and, in just twenty-three minutes of class, she changes everything. The pupils are wary of her at first, but before long they're gleefully ripping up their old textbooks and putting on new uniforms . . .

The book raises questions about nations and ideology in an abstract way, but the story's peculiar, uneasy mood makes it a great read in its own right. Takashima and I had hardly talked politics at all, but I had a feeling this book might suit his cynical personality – and more importantly, surely he hadn't already read this one?

I sent him a polite message explaining what the book was about and why I thought he'd like it, and I soon received another reply: 'This one looks interesting, I've never heard of it. I'll try and pick up a copy soon.'

I'd finally got the okay (at least, I thought so). And *of course* he hadn't been rejecting my suggestions to be mean; he really had just wanted me to introduce him to something he hadn't read. I still wasn't sure if it was quite the right choice, but never mind. Out of all my matches so far, Takashima might actually have been the one who had most wanted a book recommendation.

I would have to put more thought into how I went about choosing the books in future. It seemed obvious when I thought about it, but there would be no point in, say, recommending the new Haruki Murakami book to someone who was already an avid reader of Murakami. There had to be some key points, some basic rules for picking a book that would delight my match – maybe some kind of chart that could show me how to approach it. I thought for a while, and then took down some notes on my phone so I could look at them when I needed to.

Recommending books

- Match is well versed in a certain genre→ don't pick classic books or recent popular books from that genre.
- Match doesn't read that much→ okay to introduce famous books and classics.
- Match *does* read a lot→ classics and bestsellers basically out. Try obscure books, books they won't have heard of, genres very different from what they usually read.

- BUT you still need a reason for picking a particular book for a particular person.
- How different from their usual genre? Make overall judgement about match – will they enjoy something totally different, or just slightly?
- Book might go down better if you base it on general impression you get from match, instead of going by facts like gender, age, job, interests, etc. (Like with fortune-telling, or designing a personalised cocktail.)

That was about all I had for now. If I thought of anything else, I'd add it to the list.

*

Another evening, another meeting.

It was the first time I'd matched up with another girl. I hadn't thought I'd been particularly uncomfortable meeting men I didn't know, but now, having finally arranged to meet another woman, I realised how comfortable it was to hang out with someone of the same gender and just to be able to let your guard down.

Sayaka had recently finished uni and started her first job. She was like a doll, slender and cute, with a cheerful, good-humoured nature – just as lovely as a girl could be.

'You're so pretty, isn't it difficult using PerfectStrangers? Don't you get people hitting on you all the time?' I asked her. She had been a site member for a while, so I just had to know.

'I can easily tell when people are only on the site for *that*. When they're just trying to meet young girls, I mean,' she said. She showed the site to me on her phone as she explained. 'If you get an iffy feeling about someone, first check their profile, then look at the wish list of people they want to meet. And bingo! If it's only pictures of girls making cute faces, it's obvious.' She giggled.

To test this out, I checked the profiles of the first two men I'd met: the ones who'd extended those generous invitations to be friends with benefits. It was exactly as Sayaka had predicted; in fact, she was so spot on, I was astounded. Both men had exclusively listed girls with cutesy photos and unconventional names.

'And the ones who know what they're doing target people who've just joined the site and message them. I bet the two guys you met did that,' Sayaka said.

I was seriously impressed by the way she had quickly sussed those two out. Not only that, she even showed me the list of people she'd met and proceeded to go through them one by one for my benefit: 'Don't meet this guy, don't meet this guy, this guy's nice – oh, and I haven't met him or him, but based on what I've heard, they're probably no-nos too.'

I got the same feeling I'd had when I spoke with Ida: that while on the surface, PerfectStrangers seemed to promise that you could do whatever you liked, it was actually a miniature society built on trust and reputation. Maybe this only worked because it wasn't specifically geared towards meeting members of the opposite sex.

'Although I don't mind meeting people who're only after sex, as long as they're fun to talk to! Sadly though, the chat is usually boring,' said Sayaka, and I found myself agreeing heartily.

Sayaka and I chatted on. We fell about laughing as we shared our most ridiculous romantic experiences with each other, snorting indecorously in a way that hardly seemed appropriate in the elegant café where we'd arranged to meet.

'I always end up falling for chubby guys who can sing,' I said.

'What? Nanako, what kind of random preference is that?! I don't believe you.'

'I don't know . . . I went to a karaoke evening with some friends and there was this guy singing stuff by that boy band, Da Pump. I mean it's not like I'm even *into* Da Pump, they're awful! But the way he sang was sexy, and somehow I ended up going home with him . . . Then the next day I was like, how did I end up here? Please don't tell me Da Pump had anything to do with it?!'

'Nooo, that's tragic! I just like men who're good looking and uncomplicated. My top pick would be a foreign guy. They're just as shallow as hot Japanese guys, though – no, more, even! And they have no concept of faithfulness whatsoever! But I can't speak any English and it takes a while before I realise just how shallow they are. So the good thing with foreign guys is that the relationship lasts longer!'

'Seriously? But then it's just a matter of time!' I said.

'I know, that's why I've decided I shouldn't do stupid stuff like that anymore. So on days when I feel like I'm in danger of slipping, I wear these tacky Rilakkuma pants to try and stop myself wasting my time on the wrong guy.'

'Rilakkuma?' I said, mentally picturing a pair of pants plastered with the unsmiling face of that ubiquitous cartoon bear. 'Why do you even *have* pants like that in the first place?!'

'My friend brought them back from Thailand as a souvenir. But actually, last time I wore them to meet a guy I was too embarrassed to let him see them, so in the end I came out of the hotel shower wearing just a towel instead and went to bed like that. So my plan completely backfired! There must be a better way . . .'

And on and on we chatted, until the café closed and they turfed us out.

A few days later, I recommended Sayaka a collection of essays: *Bare Naked Girls' Talk* by Artesia. When you open the book, your gaze is immediately drawn by the sections of big, bold, eye-wateringly frank text on sexually explicit topics. Some of it is so shocking, it almost makes you want to snap the book shut again. It's not the kind of thing you can read when other people are around – definitely not one for the train. But there's a strong feminism underpinning the humorous way it talks about sex from a woman's perspective, and running through the writing is this desire for women to escape male dominance and the biases of society, to find affirmation in their own womanhood and achieve happiness for themselves through their own power, without relying on men.

Some time later, Sayaka replied to my message.

'Thanks for the rec. I got the book!! Shame I can't display it on my shelf at home! It's fab though, I agree with so much of it. Will try and keep all her lessons in mind! 🎵 I'd better have more adventures – then we can report back to each other now and again! ☆'

The message was cheerful and sweet from beginning to end, just like Sayaka. I felt my mood lift just reading it.

So there I was. I'd met Ida and Sayaka: genuinely decent, interesting people. We'd communicated well, we'd had a great time together, and I hadn't received any disappointing messages afterwards. And of course, I'd been able to introduce them to new books; in fact the books I wanted to recommend had come to me naturally while we chatted.

All this had seemed like some distant, unachievable dream at first, yet slowly but surely everything had fallen into place. Before I'd started using PerfectStrangers, I'd felt wary and uneasy at the thought of meeting people I didn't know. But now, those feelings had melted away.

*

In the end, I never met up with Ida or Sayaka again. But there *was* someone from PerfectStrangers who I stayed friends with – who I'm still friends with, in fact. His name was Endo and he was a filmmaker, three years younger than me. He worked in the trendy Harajuku district, in a shared office he'd set up with some friends.

'We're waiting for a sofa to be delivered and the office will be a bit hectic with my friends' colleagues going in and out,' his message had said. 'But would you like to visit anyway? I've got coffee, at least!'

We were scheduled to meet at three in the afternoon. I thought it might be nice to take along something to eat, so I popped into a shop in Shibuya and picked up two small tubs of Godiva ice cream before heading to Endo's office.

I'd pictured the office as being a cold, impersonal space, so I was surprised to find it actually had quite an upbeat, fun feel. There were colourful chairs and tables, and a display shelf against the wall that was home to a row of Snoopy figurines.

'Hello! Come in, make yourself at home!' Endo welcomed me in with a bashful smile and gestured towards a chair.

He was short and boyish, and he sported flashy trainers and black-rimmed glasses that all screamed Harajuku, but that suited him surprisingly well. He had a friendly smile.

I was always nervous for the first few moments of speaking to someone from PerfectStrangers, but after two or three minutes that worry would soon disappear, and my match would go from being someone I didn't know to someone I did.

Another strange thing I had discovered since joining Perfect-Strangers was that after three minutes of talking to someone – or maybe even just a minute – before we'd got into anything particularly deep, I was already able to pretty much sense whether we were going to gel, whether we'd have fun chatting to each other, what they were like as a person.

Within just a minute of meeting Endo, I thought we could be friends. In fact, I thought I might really like him.

'Here, a present.' I handed him the tubs of ice cream.

'Oh, amazing! This stuff's even posher than Häagen-Dazs! Look, the tubs are all gold and shiny. Which do you prefer, Nanako, milk chocolate or dark?'

'I like both. You pick your favourite.'

'Are you sure? Okay then – milk! I'm embarrassed to say my tastes are basically those of a child,' he laughed. He talked as though he was aware he was being cute, but he seemed genuine, and I found myself warming to him further.

'Actually, it's not just my food preferences that're like a kid's,' he said. 'I'm the same with my job. I couldn't be a salaryman or anything like that, wearing a suit and working for a big corporation. I feel like I'd die if I wasn't doing something I enjoyed. I want money too, of course, but I don't want it to become the goal. And I don't really get too gloomy or worried about life. I mean, I'm not great at thinking about things too seriously, to be honest.'

'That's sort of the impression I get from you,' I said. 'But I think that's great! I feel like you're the kind of person who's fun to be around.' I wasn't just saying it. I'd only been in the vicinity of Endo and his buoyant good cheer for a short while, but I was in unusually good spirits. I felt so relaxed around him that it was hard to believe we had only just met.

'Aww, really? That's so nice of you!' he said.

'Endo – you must like yourself, right?' I asked.

'Can you tell already? You've got me sussed out on our first meeting! That's kind of embarrassing . . . I'm only saying this because I think you'll get it, but it's true, I do really like myself. But it's more that I just want everyone to be happy, that's all. Me and the people around me,' he said.

'I think that's the best way to be. Everyone wants to be happy like that, but they can't, that's why they worry and get stressed out.'

'Hmm . . . You reckon?'

'Oh – anyway, let's eat the ice creams before they melt!' I said.

'All right! Thanks so much for bringing them!' Endo beamed radiantly, and cupped both hands together to receive the little tub of ice cream.

'So what's it like being a filmmaker? I know nothing about it,' I said.

Endo named a TV programme and asked me if I'd heard of it. 'The opening of that show, that's probably the biggest thing I've done. And then I sometimes shoot music videos for young musicians who aren't very well known. But mainly it's corporate promo videos, things like that. Just standard stuff!' he said, pulling out his phone to show me his YouTube channel. I was impressed. He was an indie filmmaker, true, but he actually seemed pretty well known.

Then he told me about why he was on PerfectStrangers, and about making films with his friends when he was a teenager. He talked about his favourite manga, the countries he'd been to, the big festival in the States called Burning Man, which was held in the desert . . . We chatted on and on, moving from one topic to the next, the conversation never drying up.

'You manage a Village Vanguard, don't you? That's amazing!'
'Well, it's not *that* amazing,' I said.
'I really like those yellow signs they stick on everything! I'd love to try writing one. And picking weird things to put in the shop!' said Endo.

It wasn't just him; when I mentioned Village Vanguard, I often got this kind of reaction. At this point, I would usually get some laughs by revealing a few funny crowd-pleasing anecdotes about the place.

For example, in any other company, being good looking or having been to a prestigious school or uni would be a plus. But not in Village Vanguard. There, you were more in danger of being saddled with a weird nickname. Right at the top of the company hierarchy was someone with the dubious accolade of having had numerous videos featured on Tamori Club, a late-night variety programme. (Part of the TV show involved amusing the host with DIY music videos featuring deliberately misheard song lyrics.) Another of the bosses was known for his unconventional fetish; everyone had heard him talk about how he'd been slapped with a raw fish by his girlfriend, and how it had been the most thrilling moment of his life. Things like that.

And then there were the stories from when I'd just become shop manager. Once, I'd left the shop in the hands of the young staff on the late shift and headed off home. I realised I'd forgotten something, so I went back to pick it up – only to find every member of staff standing behind the till eating soft-serve ice cream. I was so surprised, I couldn't even bring myself to get angry at them. They could tell it looked really bad – but we ended up in this absurd situation where none of them could put their ice creams down anywhere, and they all just had to stand to attention, straight-backed and sheepish, every one of them with a cone in their hand.

And then there was the general meeting where the company's director, with a deeply pained expression on his face, had announced, 'This year, our top-selling product across the whole company was . . . the squeezable breast ball.' These were the kinds of stories I'd entertain my matches with. Usually, at least.

I thought about sharing them with Endo, but for some reason I didn't feel like it. Instead, I found myself saying, 'It used to be fun. But it's not anymore. I want to quit.'

I was surprised at my own words. Where had *that* come from, all of a sudden? My abruptness had made me sound a little angry and I felt suddenly embarrassed, but Endo didn't seem to mind.

'Oh, really! So what are you going to do next?' he said, as though it was the most natural thing in the world.

Hang on – that was a pretty big deal, what I'd just said. Endo was being so casual about the idea of quitting, but Village

Vanguard was my life! This wasn't just someone moaning about how they wanted to leave some old company they'd only been at for a couple of years; this was *different*.

But then I realised that from someone else's perspective, actually, there really was no difference at all, and I wondered why I was clinging on to the place so desperately. I wished I could be casual about it too. The kind of person who just thought, *So, what's next then?*

Endo was full of this bubbly levity, this positivity. And I knew I had it inside me too, deep down, but I felt like it was starting to ebb away. At that moment, for some reason, I felt certain that I'd be able to get it back somehow if I was around Endo. I'd be able to be the me I wanted to be.

'You're great, Endo, you're so positive. I mean, I feel like you don't get jealous of other people, or say bad things about them, or anything. I didn't think I was that negative a person, but you're on a whole other level. I wish I was more like you!'

'You think? That's really nice of you! But it's not true – I see friends on Facebook or wherever succeeding in business and getting their new houses built, and I always think, *You're so annoying! I hope you fail at something!*' Endo declared with refreshing honesty. He grinned, and I looked at his smiling face and thought, *I really, really like him.*

We'd been talking for about two hours when a big delivery was brought in, probably the sofa, and some other people came in to the office and started working away in the next room.

Our conversation suddenly broke off. Endo hadn't given any indication that he wanted to finish up, but I wondered if I was now keeping him from his work. I was just thinking how I still wanted to talk to him a little bit longer, when he said, 'Anyway... let's think of something to talk about next!'

I was a little relieved, but I also felt like accepting his somewhat contrived suggestion at face value might be sort of like tacitly agreeing to something. So, slightly forcedly, I reached for some fairly trivial topic of conversation.

'Oh yeah, the manga we were talking about earlier, that reminds me...'

A little while later, Endo looked at the Mac that had been open beside him all this time and said, 'Someone should be sending me some work stuff in the next half hour or so. Once I've checked it, I can finish up for the day, so do you want to get dinner together?'

'Really? That would be great!'

And so we sallied forth into the city, the light already beginning to fade, and went into a smoke-filled back-street yakiniku barbecue restaurant. We'd been chatting for hours now, but there was still so much I wanted to talk about. After we'd eaten, we moved to a cramped bar inside a small building and drank until it was time for the last train home. Before we parted, we added each other on the LINE app, and at the station ticket gates we said our goodbyes with a smile.

'I had a great time. See you again!' I said.

'Me too. I'll message you!' said Endo.

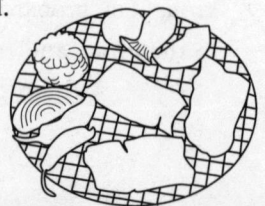

I headed off down the escalator, walking a little quicker than normal. As I was making my way through the subway tunnel, my phone, still clasped in my hand, vibrated and a LINE notification appeared on the screen.

'I suddenly felt lonely when you left. Do you want to hang out till morning?'

I gazed at the message for a moment, and then spun around and jumped on the escalator going back up.

When I got back to the ticket gates, Endo was waiting there, waving at me without a trace of embarrassment, as though we'd had this meeting arranged all along. And yet, neither of us seemed to me to be the sort of person that would have an unspoken agreement to spend the night at a hotel.

'Well . . . I'm glad we've joined forces again, but what shall we do?' I said.

'Good point. Hmm . . . Oh, fancy a game of darts? Though I haven't played for years.'

So we went to play darts for a bit, and then we went to Hub for another drink. They were showing football on TV, which we watched for a while. When we tired of that, we started playing phone games, and then got chatting again. By now we were speaking completely openly with each other, and I was so comfortable around Endo that it seemed like we had been friends all our lives. We idly frittered away the hours together, and it felt like one of those lazy, hazy summer holidays that goes on forever. And then I started to feel a faint drowsiness creep over me.

'Hey, Nanako!'

'Um? Uh . . . yes?'

'Sorry, I'm actually getting super sleepy. I feel bad, it was me who said we should hang out till morning in the first place. Want to take a nap in the office till the trains start up again?'

'What? Oh, um, sure . . .' I said.

What did he mean by that? Was he asking me . . . you know? I looked at him and tried to gauge his intentions. There'd been no suggestion of anything like that so far, so maybe he didn't mean much by it after all.

And anyway, was that how I wanted things to be with him? Or wasn't it? I could see myself in twenty minutes or so being pushed to make a decision.

I thought about it all the while as the two of us walked back to the office, but when we arrived I still didn't have an answer. I liked Endo, no doubt about that, but did I want a romantic relationship with him? I didn't really know. And I also felt it would be a shame if we hooked up and then things got awkward, and we ended up drifting away from each other instead . . .

Endo was blissfully ignorant of my worries. As soon as he entered the office, he said, 'Oh, the sofa's all set up! Woohoo!' and toppled onto it. He didn't seem to be getting up again. Was he waiting for me to react? Or for something else? For me to ask if I could join him on the sofa? I hung back, sizing up the situation. Moments later, the sound of snoring reached my ears.

Oh well. I bedded down on the rug and helped myself to a book from the shelves. I loved extraordinary nights like these – they made me feel like I was on a journey somewhere.

I was just beginning to nod off when it was time for the trains to start running again. I ventured back out into the streets with Endo and found it was lighter than I'd realised it would be outside. It had been a long time since I'd seen the city at dawn. Crows flew leisurely, swooping low, pecking at the translucent bin bags that sat there on the pavement waiting to be collected. How long had it been since I'd seen the sky this particular shade of dark blue, and experienced the heavy drowsiness that came with pulling an all-nighter? *It feels just like being seventeen again*, I thought, as the two of us walked towards the subway steps.

It was slightly embarrassing standing facing one another again at the ticket gates where we'd said goodbye only five hours ago.

'Have you got work today?' Endo asked.

'Yeah. I can go home and get a couple of hours of sleep, maybe. How about you?'

'I've got a meeting at ten, so I'll go home first and get changed. Not sure if it's worth trying to get any sleep.'

'Oh, right. Well . . . see you.'

'Yeah.'

Was this where we should kiss? Or just leave things like that? Was there something more I should say? All these questions flashed through my mind at once. After a moment of hesitation, I hugged Endo briefly, and we parted.

It was such an indifferent, nothing decision. Maybe we could have kissed after all, I thought, or even had sex last night; maybe no matter what I'd decided, we would have wound up here in the end anyway.

I boarded the train, took my phone out of my bag again and looked at it. No LINE messages this time. I wavered a bit, and then, though it wasn't particularly worth mentioning, I sent: 'That's me on the train. Thanks for spending so much time with me, I had fun!' The message immediately showed as read, and then came a short reply: 'Me too! See you again.' That was all.

I sat there, swaying back and forth on the train in a treacle-like torpor, and recalled to mind everything that had happened. I didn't know how I felt about it all, and I didn't know how Endo felt about it either. Was I going to develop serious feelings for him? At some point down the road, would we actually end up going out with each other?

It felt like ages since I'd imagined something like that happening to me. It seemed like a bright enough future, and yet somehow I struggled to picture it.

Was it all right for me to develop feelings for someone? I mean, what was I going to do about my husband?

I had no idea. I just didn't know. And yet, I had the sensation that slowly, slowly, a new life was opening up before me.

The book I recommended to Endo was *Mojacko* by Fujiko F Fujio. I'd picked it because he said he wanted to read an interesting sci-fi manga. It was fair to say I didn't know that much about hardcore sci-fi manga, but I did think this was Fujiko F Fujio's best work, and I definitely wanted Endo to read it, if he hadn't already.

Mojacko is a masterpiece. It was originally serialised in a magazine aimed at older primary-school kids, but the subject matter is quite grown up; it's packed with knotty social issues like suicide, brainwashing and religion, all rolled up in a rollicking space adventure. Plus, I knew Endo liked hip hop and was a fan of the group Rhymester, and Utamaru from Rhymester was also a Fujiko F Fujio fan. In his afterword in the author's collected works, Utamaru declares that *Mojacko* is the best (as I do). So all in all, the perfect pick for Endo, I thought.

Endo had told me he didn't buy books in hard copy, but some time later he sent me a short message: 'Thanks, I got it on Amazon! It was really great!'

*

I was in a veritable frenzy of meeting new people, but all the while I was still seeing my husband about once a month, too. Even though we no longer lived together, we met up for dinner every so often to try and find a peaceful resolution to our situation. But both of us were scared to get to the heart of the matter, and we danced around it, chatting about trivial things instead. It felt somehow that if we went to normal restaurants we wouldn't really enjoy ourselves, so we meaninglessly dined out at slightly fancier places, even though we weren't celebrating anything.

I wondered whether there was any point in us eating together like this. But trying to change things felt like a huge deal, and I couldn't bring myself to do anything about it. All I wanted was not to have to make a decision. And every time after dinner, when we parted at the station as though we were nothing more than friends, I was left with an inexpressible sense of fatigue weighing on my heart.

I didn't like the vague, inarticulate person I was with my husband, or the indecisive ditherer who complained that she wanted to quit her job but never actually tried to do it. I preferred the person I was when I was using PerfectStrangers, impulsively facing the unknown – even though a part of me still wanted to laugh at myself for it, because it was such an odd thing to do, after all.

*

More and more now, I found myself matching up with people who seemed genuinely lovely. I wasn't sure if it was just coincidence, or if it was because my own credibility had improved – or perhaps I was getting better at finding that kindness in people and drawing it out of them.

One such person was Nao.

In the world of PerfectStrangers, a veritable pandemonium crawling with all manner of ghoulies and ghosties and long-legged beasties, Nao was like a wildflower blooming in the wilderness. A soft, cuddly girl with a sunny disposition, she had recently left her long-term job and was getting ready to go it alone as a freelance photographer.

Nao was cheerful, she was kind, she was a good listener, a positive thinker, a hard worker. Though she was totally different to Sayaka, again I found that just being with another girl meant I could relax and open up more, and we chatted away merrily. Even in the short time we were together, she was quick to compliment me on the way I spoke, my ideas, the way I thought – things I wouldn't even have noticed myself.

'Nana-chan, that's what's so great about you!' she kept saying, with complete sincerity. It felt like she had some divine gift, a natural power of affirmation, and I was wholeheartedly drawn to her.

So that was Nao. And then there was Yukari, whom Nao told me I just *had* to meet. Yukari was a life coach and if you met her, Nao said, she would give you a free coaching session.

'What exactly is life coaching?' I asked Nao. 'Is it like self-affirmation or something? You know, looking in the mirror and going, "You can do it! You can do it!" Isn't it kind of a scam?'

'Hah, Nana-chan, what are you on about? It's okay, it's nothing scammy! It's just about understanding what it is you really want.'

And so it was that I soon found myself meeting Yukari. She was waiting for me in Tully's Coffee near the west exit of Shinjuku Station, sitting right at the back. Her gentle voice and warm smile put me at ease as soon as we'd exchanged a few words.

Once we'd briefly introduced ourselves and shared more or less what had brought us here, Yukari gave me a basic explanation of life coaching.

'It often gets confused with counselling – but where a counsellor listens to you, helps you get things in order and suggests some solutions, I'd say coaching is more about you realising things and deciding things for yourself.'

'But how are you going to understand things about yourself if you can't understand them by yourself, if you see what I mean?' I said. I was somewhat dubious about the whole thing, but I supposed I could see the need for someone else's involvement if it helped you find your own way to the answers.

'Why don't we actually give it a go?' Yukari said. 'You already told me a little bit about where you're at now, Nanako. Could you tell me what it is that's worrying you most at the moment?'

'Well . . . it's not something that's really worrying me, exactly, but I have no idea about what I want to do next. I don't even know whether I want to split from my husband or give things another go, so I thought I'd give it a year to just see how things go before making a decision. And with work . . . I do vaguely feel like I want to quit, but I don't know what else I want to be, or what I want to do next.'

I felt apologetic for bringing up these wishy-washy concerns – after all, it wasn't as though I was seriously agonising over these things – but I decided to take Yukari up on her offer all the same.

'Okay,' she said. 'Well, let's get started.'

'Close your eyes . . .' said Yukari. 'All right, Nanako, now I want you to imagine yourself alone in the middle of a big, wide room. You're standing on a square tile about a metre across, and it's a different colour from the rest of the floor. That tile represents you, as you are now. How do you feel at the moment, standing there? It's all right if you can't sum up your feelings perfectly, or if you can't quite find the right words – anything's okay. Just say whatever comes to mind.'

'I feel anxious,' I said.

'Anxious in what way?'

'It's just a kind of vague feeling . . .'

'Okay, so it's a vague anxiety. Try having a little think about what might be causing it,' said Yukari.

'Not knowing what to do next . . .' I said.

That obviously wasn't really it. I didn't have any good answers. But then all of a sudden it was like a switch had been flipped, and the words surged up and came tumbling out of my mouth.

'I have friends, and my job's not all bad, and I've had lots of things to enjoy, but . . . I mean, it's the same with my marriage, too – I feel like I'm going to lose everything, like I'm going to be left with nothing . . .'

'I see. So you're anxious because it feels like you'll have nothing left,' Yukari said.

'Yes. But I think that would actually be fine. I don't *want* to cling on and cling on to things forever just because I'm scared of them disappearing. It's just . . . I can't see myself ever finding anything good to replace them with, like a job I want to do, or a person I want to be with.'

As I spoke, I was shocked to find that tears were running down my cheeks.

'I hardly have any friends from my uni days,' I continued. 'My job's full of eccentrics and I've always really thrived in that environment. If I leave the company I won't be able to manage among "normal" people. I've always been like that. It's not that I don't want to make myself fit in with everyone, it's that I really can't. That's why I haven't been able to get up the nerve to quit . . . If I can't be with my colleagues anymore, I won't have a place to be myself. The work and the people were so right for me that Village Vanguard is basically my whole identity now. And that's been a really good thing in my life. But now I'm starting to feel like it can't last much longer. I don't think I can do it . . . How can I leave a job that's been so much to me? How can I find something else I'll enjoy as much as I've enjoyed it in the past . . .?'

The tears flowed on, and now I was almost wailing. What was this? Was I all right? Was I emotionally unstable? Had I been hypnotised or something? No, surely it wasn't that easy; you couldn't hypnotise someone just by getting them to stand on an imaginary square. Yet here I was, howling, in a crowded coffee shop, in front of someone I'd only just met. It was absolutely mortifying. What should I do?

'Sorry, I'm sorry . . . I can't stop crying . . .'

'That's all right. If you feel like you can talk, then keep going.'

There were things I wanted to say, but I was heaving with sobs, my breathing constricted, and I struggled to talk normally. The harder I tried to get the words out, the more the tears flowed. Yukari seemed like she was used to all this. She didn't look at all surprised or put out; she just continued to talk to me with quiet composure.

'Okay, now five metres in front of you, there's another tile, the same colour. Let's try walking over there. I want you to go and stand on that tile, just like you did with the first one.'

While I cried, the calmer side of me was impressed by how these imaginary tiles could be so effective. In my mind, I followed Yukari's instructions and walked over to the other tile.

'This is the place where you will be a year from now,' said Yukari. 'You've managed to become the you that you want to be in a year's time. What's that like for you, Nanako? How do you feel?'

'The me I want to be . . . in a year . . .?'

This time, my words suddenly dried up. I didn't know what sort of me I wanted to be. I thought for a while, but nothing came out.

Yukari continued to encourage me, rewording the question again and again.

'What does the scenery around you look like? What kind of people are there around you? Can you see anything, can you hear anything? Is there anything you feel now, that maybe you didn't feel before?'

An image suddenly rose to my mind unbidden, and I pushed it away at once. It was a mistake to base your own happiness on other people. It had to be rooted in yourself; it had to be able to stand alone.

'I did think of something for a moment just now. But I don't think it's quite right, so . . . um . . .' I faltered.

'There's no right and wrong to what you're thinking. It's okay if you think it's something other people wouldn't approve of, or if it's something strange. After all, it could be that thing you really want finally revealing itself to you.'

For some reason, I still felt hugely reluctant to voice my thoughts. Yukari waited patiently for a good long while. After some time, I managed to force out a few words.

'I'm . . . surrounded by really nice people, enjoying myself. More than I am now.'

'Well, that sounds really wonderful, doesn't it?' Yukari said.

Oh, she's right! I thought. *It's not that strange at all. Why didn't I want to say it?* It was an odd sensation, as though the words had taken on an entirely different meaning somewhere on the way from my brain to my mouth. Until I'd actually said it out loud, I'd felt like there was something pathetic about the idea of trying to make things better for yourself by somehow relying on the niceness of others, on the feeling you got from the people around you. I'd been ashamed, and felt like I was useless for even thinking it.

'Now, I'd like to ask you a little bit more about that thought,' said Yukari. 'Did you get any sense of what it was about those people that was so nice?'

'They don't just complain about work, they're not defeatist all the time. They really take pleasure in their jobs, and live with a free spirit, and are forward-looking, and find out about new things – and instead of being stylish and good looking and dressing head to toe in branded stuff, their fashion choices are weird, baffling even, but that's what actually makes them so cool . . . Something like that . . .'

The floodgates opened again while the other, calmer side of me looked on. I had no idea what I was talking about anymore, especially that bit at the end about the clothes – but I supposed that must be my heart's desire. To be friends with people with questionable fashion sense, or something.

'I think that's really lovely. Okay, let's make this the last one. When you're surrounded by these people, Nanako, why do you feel you enjoy it so much?'

It was just a simple, straightforward question, and yet the words seemed to stab at me like daggers, causing my tears to flow unstoppably.

'B-Because I've become someone who . . . who can hang out with people like that as, as an equal . . . N-Not like I am now . . .'

I was back to bawling. Once again, I no longer had any idea what I was saying.

Looking back, I'd never been that good at talking about myself.

I'd act like everything was fine and dandy, like I was having fun. I'd take pains to be bright and breezy. It was partly because I wanted to make it look as though my life was going well, and partly because even if I did want to talk to people about how hard things were, I had this deeply ingrained feeling that I should hold back.

It'll just be awkward for them, I would think. *No one wants to have to hear this stuff, it's not fun.*

And so I was in the habit of telling people I was doing fine, telling them I was enjoying myself. Even I had always believed that I meant it.

The coaching session ended, and Yukari waited for me to regain my composure. In an attempt to cover up my embarrassment, I asked her some more about life coaching and we chit-chatted a little before leaving Tully's. As we headed to Shinjuku Station, Yukari mentioned that she was going home to coach another client on Skype.

'Do you do it as your job, then?' I asked.

'Yes. This client pays forty thousand yen for three sessions, and we've been working together for a while.'

That's not cheap! I thought. But when I considered how much I'd cried my eyes out just in today's short session, I felt perhaps that the price was fair.

'You coached me for free today, though,' I said. 'So do you do something different when you're with paying clients?'

'No, there's no difference.'

'Really? Um . . . Sorry if this sounds rude, but do you do the free sessions for people on PerfectStrangers to advertise your coaching work?'

'Well . . . If people like it, of course, then I'm very happy to take them on as paying clients. But that's not really why I do it – I just like it! I like coaching people, it's what I want to do whether I get paid or not.'

I'd never seen anyone approach their work like this before, and it had a powerful impact on me. It was a while before I managed to fully digest the idea.

Once I got home, I mulled over Yukari's words some more. We all had to balance the equation between work, money and whatever it was we loved to do. We all had to solve that for ourselves, and live according to whatever answer we came up with.

I'd often seen people who wanted to turn the thing they loved into their work, and had to get themselves into a position where they could make their passion pay. If they weren't well enough established, they would work for free at first and build up a reputation, then get their customers to advertise their business by word of mouth.

And then there were those who decided they weren't skilled enough yet, so they provided their services for free as a means of getting experience. On the flip side, there were plenty of people who pursued their passion because they enjoyed it, and didn't mind if it wasn't profitable.

Yukari seemed to love life coaching from the bottom of her heart, and I really believed she would be doing it whether or not she was paid. That must be what it meant to find your calling.

It would be nice not to have to think about the business side of things, or monetisation, certainly – but that wasn't why I was so interested. I just thought it would be wonderful if I could face the world feeling the same way Yukari did.

What was my calling? Could I really only find it in Village Vanguard? Was it working in a bookshop? Or perhaps the issue was something more fundamental – if didn't have anywhere I could be myself, maybe I just needed a place where I could get by, somehow. But I was well beyond my self-centred teenage years now, and the world didn't revolve around me anymore. I wanted to be of use to other people too, just like Yukari.

This was my message to her:

'Hi Yukari, thank you so much for the coaching session the other day. I'm really sorry I cried so much! But you helped me take a look at the real cause of my anxiety, even though I hadn't recognised it myself. It was a big shock for me, but I think I understand things better now. The way you think about your job also gave me a lot of food for thought, so thank you for that, too. My new goal is to be able to go to work with the same attitude as you.

'I'd like to recommend you the book *What Did You Eat?* by Hiromi Ito and Nahomi Edamoto. It's a really wonderful book; it's a record of the correspondence between the two women: a poet and a celebrity chef, both in their forties. Late at night in their quiet kitchens, they write down their thoughts and fax them to each other – their dilemmas about work, family, raising children, romance . . . I was only about twenty when I first read it, and I remember finding it so weird imagining I would still have all these worries even when I was a proper adult.

'But as I've got older, I've found myself thinking that rather than being a grown-up with no worries, it's actually more wonderful to be facing your life even while you *are* dealing with that stuff, and laughing and crying with your girlfriends, and really just living life as best you can.

'I think the book contains some of the same strength and kindness that I got from you when we talked. It's a book that makes me feel it's good to be alive. Plus, in between the bits about the authors' everyday lives, there are lists of the things they had for dinner, and recipes for food they cooked and enjoyed, so you really feel like you're right there with them! I hope you'll give it a read.'

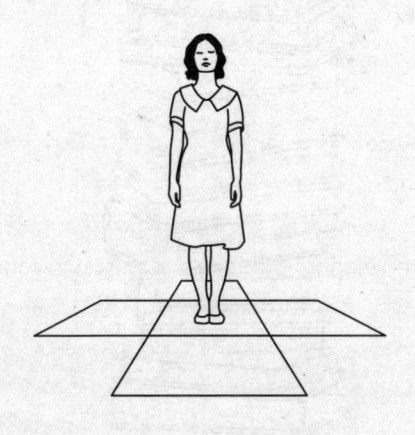

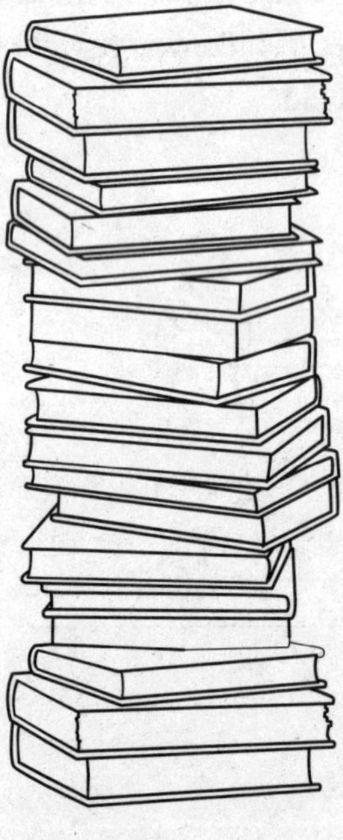

CHAPTER 4

PEOPLE IN TRANSIT

Since I'd started meeting people through PerfectStrangers, it was the world outside work, outside Village Vanguard, that had become the richer, more colourful part of my life. When I met someone from outside work on my days off, I found my mood improved. Back in the shop, though, the tedium of the daily grind was waiting: the incessant complaints by the part-timers; new poorly thought-out measures that someone or other had decided we had to rush out across the whole company; and conversations with colleagues who'd become used to pointing out with cynical relish that it didn't matter what we did, because it never made a difference anyway.

It wasn't as though any of this was new, and yet until now I'd never seriously thought about quitting. It was partly because I liked my colleagues and Village Vanguard itself and didn't want to leave them behind, and partly because I thought I wouldn't find anywhere better – that I wasn't capable of doing anything else.

But Endo's cheerful question – 'So what are you going to do next?' – had given me pause for thought. And then I'd met Yukari and bawled my eyes out. And I'd been recommending books to my matches, and delighting them or not delighting them, as the case may be – but either way, every time, I'd sat there grinning from ear to ear as I typed out my message, thinking what a perfect fit the book would be . . . All these things were nudging me millimetre by millimetre towards the water's edge. I no longer knew why I'd been so convinced I could never quit Village Vanguard, even though I wanted to.

I had reached the point where it was really the only option. If I didn't leave, if I stayed where I was, I couldn't see myself in a year's time ending up in that lovely place Yukari had shown me. But if I did leave, what next? I had no answer. And so I just couldn't do it.

I wished, I *wished* I could keep meeting people and picking books for them like I was doing now, and that it would somehow pay the bills. Was that impossible? In the meantime, I kept going on PerfectStrangers, matching with person after person after person like an obsession. Meeting strangers had become part of my life now.

When I had a day off coming up, I'd log on to PerfectStrangers the day before and check if anyone interesting had listed a chat. If they had, I would respond to it. If not, I'd list my own. It was easier to find people to meet in central Tokyo, in places like Shibuya and Shinjuku, rather than out in Yokohama, so I'd make plans to pop into a certain bookshop or go bargain hunting in Shinjuku while I was there, and then set my meeting time and place accordingly. It was good because it forced me to get out of the flat by a particular time, which meant I couldn't squander my days off idling about at home.

Maeno was a medical student. He was on track to become a doctor, but was having doubts about where he was headed.

'I'm interested in medicine itself, and I do still want to do research and things. But the world of medicine is kind of insular – the system is so old school, and I just don't think it'll suit me,' he said. 'I see my high-school friends talking about starting their own businesses or going off to build schools in Africa, and I feel so jealous. Like I want to do something like that too. And this is a different thing altogether, but I was also thinking I'd like to travel the world before starting work. So I've been reading lots of blogs by people who're travelling.'

My first impression of Maeno had been that of a typical A-grade medical student, so I was a little surprised to hear he was interested in that kind of thing.

'I went to this talk by someone who'd travelled the world, and they gave me some Zambian banknotes as a souvenir,' he said. 'I thought, "Wow, I'd better keep these for something special!" and that's when I had my idea.'

'Ooh, what was it?' I asked.

'Do you know that folk tale about the straw millionaire? The peasant who starts with a piece of straw and then trades it for something better, and then something even better . . . I was thinking, why don't *I* do that? I could start off with the Zambian banknotes and exchange them with people I meet for better and better things. And make my end goal a round-the-world plane ticket. And then I'll go off travelling.'

'Oh, that sounds amazing!'

It was the first time I'd met another person who had thought up their own hook for using PerfectStrangers. 'Actually, I'm making a book recommendation for everyone I meet on the site! It's kind of similar,' I said.

'Oh yeah! You know, I think I always want to push the boundaries,' said Maeno. 'It would be boring using PerfectStrangers without changing things up a bit. I mean, I *could* just work away at a part-time job, and I could buy plane tickets to travel the world, no problem. But that wouldn't be very interesting. I wanted to find a way to take it up a level.'

'Well, why not? I guess you're just doing things your way. I think it's a great idea. Oh – so what's happened to the Zambian currency now?' I asked.

'I traded it for a bottle opener, then a lightweight folding umbrella, then a toaster, then a digital camera, and right now I've got a suitcase. I should have brought it with me, but never mind . . .'

'Wow! You've managed to make loads of trades, then! Just like the straw millionaire.' I found myself wanting to take part too, and I rummaged around in my bag, but of course I had nothing to exchange that would rank higher than a suitcase.

'Only people who've tried trading up would understand, I think, but this is where it gets tricky. It starts getting really hard to make swaps,' Maeno told me.

That made sense. But I also found the idea funny, in a way – *was* there really a community of people who could sympathise with each other about the trials and tribulations of trading up? Something about the way Maeno was taking it all so seriously made me want to help him.

'I wonder if there's anything else you could do to find swaps,' I said. 'Could you increase the number of items, maybe? Trade the suitcase for a hundred keyrings or something? They might be easier to exchange. But then a pile of keyrings is just junk, really, isn't it . . .?'

'Yeah . . . Actually, I was wondering too whether it might be better to split it into different items . . .'

Maeno and I chatted away, laughing as we bounced around various ideas and weighed up the pros and cons. It was lovely to feel included in his journey. When I asked him about books, he told me he loved *Midnight Express* and *Into the Wild*, and read them again and again to whet his appetite for travelling. So I knew my recommendation just had to be Jack Kerouac's *On the Road*. That story of young people who reject a normal life to embrace the freedom of travel was published back in the 1950s, but it still had many fans today. When Maeno went off to travel the world, I was sure the book would enrich his journey through America – and I thought the story would resonate with him, this young man who couldn't bring himself to settle down as a doctor.

*

Maki had originally worked for a publisher of language-learning materials, but had quit and was now teaching English at a cram school and ghostwriting language-study books.

'I get why there are ghostwriters for celebrity books and things, but I didn't know there were ghostwriters for language learning,' I said.

'Yep, there are!' he told me. 'Any field with famous people in it will have ghostwriters. The author of the book I'm working on right now is really arrogant, though, just awful, so I can't wait to be done with the job. And then I'd like to write my own book – that's the dream.'

'A book about language learning?'

'Yeah. Do you know TOEIC?'

'The English-language test? I know of it. I've never taken it, though,' I said.

'Well – I absolutely love it!' Maki said with a winning smile. *Okay, that's odd . . .* But then again, that was why it was fun meeting people through PerfectStrangers. Maki's cheerful mood was infectious.

'That's an interesting take on it,' I said. 'I mean, it's an English test . . . Is it the kind of thing you can really get excited about?'

'Yes – some people really like TOEIC! Including me, of course. We're called TOEICers, and there are actually quite a few of us. I take the test pretty much every time they hold it, I have done for the last five years. My goal is to score full marks every time.'

'Seriously? That's mad! There can't be many people getting full marks, surely? I don't know much about it, but I heard employers usually only ask for a score of around 700.'

'No, it's true – getting a perfect score isn't easy. I manage it about half the time. I can consistently get around 970, but full marks is a struggle. And that's why I do it! I guess it's a bit like mountaineering, in that sense.'

'If you're already scoring that highly, though, surely your language ability isn't in question?'

'True. I think I'm a perfectionist, though. I like to do things one hundred per cent,' Maki said. 'And if I do get to the stage where I can score full marks every time, I'll be able to use that as a professional selling point. There's always more to learn, so I still spend two hours a day studying.'

What was it that cheered me up so much about meeting these people who followed their own unshakeable convictions, who lived by a different set of values from everyone else? Maki was probably only doing what he enjoyed, but I found myself thrilled just hearing about it.

'I would love to speak English, but I never study at all,' I said. 'Um . . . Sorry if this is a lame question, but do you have any tips for how to keep at it?'

'That's something a lot of people struggle with,' said Maki. 'Basically, you have to make it into a habit somehow. Just like brushing your teeth. You don't go, "Hmm, should I brush my teeth? What should I do, shall I give it a miss today?" Once you're doing it every day, you don't even think about it. That's all there is to it, really. Though I know for most people it's much easier said than done.'

It was really just common sense, but it still felt like an insurmountable challenge to me, so I just nodded along as Maki spoke.

'I mean, how do you manage to read so many books, Nanako?' he asked. 'Is it because you're really motivated, or have super-strong willpower? Probably not, right?'

'No, you're right. I suppose it's more just that reading is part of my life. Books are entertainment, though – I read them because I really want to, I can't stop myself. I don't think it's the same with studying.'

'Well, that's how I feel about TOEIC!' said Maki.

I always found it so energising meeting people who were putting their heart and soul into their passions. It made me think, *I want to be like that.*

During the course of our conversation it transpired that Maki and I were the same age and, for whatever reason, we bonded over the idea that *this* was the springtime of our lives: now that we were adults, rather than in our teens or twenties. The way Maki aimed high, sparing no effort in pursuit of his goals, made me think he'd definitely enjoy a Zoonie Yamada book, so I recommended *The Grown-Ups' Short-Essay Course.*

The book is a compilation of Zoonie's email exchanges with her readers, in which she takes a fresh look at some questions with no easy answers – What is work? What is it you want to do?

What is communication? – and teaches you what an amazing thing it is to never stop asking honest questions as you move forwards through life. I thought it would be of use to Maki when he wanted to dig deeper into himself – and it might even help him at work, too, when talking to his students and listening to their concerns.

*

It was the most fascinating thing in the world to meet people I would never have encountered in my day-to-day life, and to listen to them talk about things I'd never have heard of otherwise. I was still agonising over my own work situation, which might have been why I was so struck by hearing about all these different people's experiences.

Generally speaking, most PerfectStrangers users were either tech workers, entrepreneurs or freelancers. No one else really did anything like manage a chain book-slash-novelty shop, so my matches tended to be surprised by my job, which was refreshing. I had never imagined anyone would think of me as unusual for working in a shop. And then conversely, if I happened to match with a run-of-the-mill salaryman, I'd be the one thinking *he* was unusual; I'd ask something along the lines of, 'How come a normal person like you is on PerfectStrangers?' and would be met with an awkward chuckle and a response of, 'Hang on, I could ask you the same question!'

There were also plenty of people who, when I actually met them, turned out to be different from what I'd imagined from their profiles. Everyone exaggerated their image on social media, of course – especially entrepreneurs – but still, each meeting brought home to me the fact that you couldn't really know someone at all until you met them in person. That was why I wasn't interested in trying to recommend books to people I'd only ever spoken to online.

Taguchi, for example, looked like he might be confident, a real player. His PerfectStrangers profile read: 'Student/future entrepreneur. Let's pool our knowledge and make some magic! ☆'

We matched up, and I saw that for some reason he'd listed Renoir as the meeting place. When I arrived late at the old-fashioned, upmarket café, he stood up and executed a ninety-degree bow, like a businessman greeting a client. He seemed excessively courteous and formal – the exact opposite of what I'd expected from his profile. Once we'd said our hellos, I tentatively brought this up.

'Um, it sort of feels like we're here on business or something. What's that all about? I mean, I'm not a client, you don't really need to bow to me like that.'

'Oh, right. Is that weird? Was it rude?' he said.

'No, I mean – it was extremely polite! But it's not like this is work.'

'I suppose you're right,' he said. 'But you never know what might lead to a job. I don't know about you, but I'm trying to network so I can start my own business, and I'm hoping to meet people who might want to work with me. So I want to make sure I look really reliable. That's why I picked Renoir for our meeting, too. I mean, if you were looking to hire an assistant for ten thousand yen a day, would you ask the guy waiting in McDonald's drinking a hundred-yen Fanta?'

That's not what I would base my decision on, I thought. But then I concluded that perhaps that was how things worked in the circles Taguchi wanted to move in, so I decided not to question it any further.

So that he could afford to drink coffee in Renoir, however, Taguchi was getting up at five to work in the fruit and veg section of a supermarket before going to uni, so he was chronically sleep deprived.

'But I don't want to talk about being half asleep, chopping vegetables in a supermarket. It makes me sound so poor!' he said. 'I want to present myself as a skilled entrepreneur. Sharp and capable.'

'I don't know, I think the fact you're hard-working is actually more impressive,' I said.

I wasn't sure if Taguchi's endeavour would work out for him, but I didn't think it was totally ridiculous. I'd made my debut on PerfectStrangers as Little Miss Quirky, after all, imagining that this might be the perfect place to remake myself. Perhaps the site was a testing ground where you could be who you wanted to be, try on your aspirations for size. I wanted to support Taguchi in some way. After all, he reminded me of how I had been not so long ago.

I recommended him Keiya Mizuno's *Beauty and the Beast: How to Be the Beast*. It's ostensibly a manual of dating techniques, and its jokey tone makes it a hoot from cover to cover. But while the book is chock-full of humour, the author also has this almost overly sincere side that keeps peeking through, and that eventually reveals itself at the end. I'd seen that same earnestness in Taguchi, so I wanted him to experience this masterpiece.

*

Ami was small and beautiful, a pretty girl who looked good in a pair of hotpants. The slight sugary quality of her voice and her little-girl-lost vibe made me think she'd have plenty of admirers, but there was a hint of something anxious and dark there, too. I noticed several scars on her wrists. When she began to talk to me, it was with the openness and affability you often see in people who've been through the wringer.

'I lost everything. I'm actually on welfare right now,' she told me.

She'd run away from her violent boyfriend three months ago with help from a friend, and she didn't even have any household belongings, let alone a place to live. Worse still, her boyfriend was the manager of the izakaya bar where she'd worked, so now she had no job, either. She was scared he'd find out where she was, so she couldn't contact her colleagues at the bar or post anything careless online that would reveal her whereabouts. And her boyfriend had been managing her savings, ostensibly for their wedding, and now she couldn't withdraw any of the money.

PEOPLE IN TRANSIT

It was a fairly dire situation.

'But I couldn't stay at my friend's place forever, and me and my parents don't get on, so I had no one to help me and I kind of ended up homeless,' she told me. 'You know, when I started on PerfectStrangers, I was moving from place to place and staying with girls I met through the site! I was so grateful, they were all totally open and generous even though we were complete strangers. I mean, with no money and nowhere to live, you assume your only option is to go into sex work or something, right? Or to borrow from a loan shark and rent a place to stay – though you'd never pay them back working normal part-time jobs. But I met this girl on PerfectStrangers called Chika, and she told me I might be able to get government help. And now I'm going to this college to train for a job in care, and I've been given somewhere to stay. I'm living on my own now – I'm living the dream!'

'Oh, really? That's amazing! I knew about welfare, but I didn't realise they could actually give you a job and a place to live,' I said.

'Right! Who knew? And there I was, on the verge of making my debut as a sex worker.'

Ami and I got along really well. The more we talked, the more cheerful she became and the more she seemed to enjoy herself. My own circumstances were nothing like as tough as hers, but still, we shared something in that we were both curiously upbeat despite being in situations where most people would feel sorry for us. Maybe it was just my imagination, but I felt like on

PerfectStrangers there was none of this unspoken expectation that people suffering from misfortune should have the grace to look unhappy.

Ami wanted to read something dark, something like a knife in the heart, that would completely sweep her away. I recommended George Akiyama's *Undiscardable People*. I'd found it so shocking on my first read that in the immediate aftermath it was all I could think about. The manga depicts a sex-obsessed man with absolutely no redeeming features: one half of a couple who find the rug pulled from under them the more they struggle to be happy. And yet it's a profound work, a paean to humanity in its unconditional acceptance of anyone, no matter who they are. I also knew what it was like when only the darkest of books could help lift you up, and I hoped my choice would provide Ami with some solace.

Everyone you met on PerfectStrangers was in transit, on their way to somewhere else. If someone, say, loved their work, their family and relationships were ticking along well, and they were satisfied and happy just the way they were, then you wouldn't find them here. No – people on PerfectStrangers had just quit their job; or they were approaching one of life's turning points, like starting their own business or shifting career; or they were uneasy about themselves the way they were, and felt that something had to change.

It seemed to me as though we were all politely giving each other a glimpse of our insecurities, lowering our guards just a little and allowing others to get close. But then again, wasn't that just how the whole of society worked?

In each thirty-minute encounter, you listened to the digest of someone else's life and offered up your own condensed life in turn. It was fun to see how deep you could go in that limited time. It was like free diving to the bottom of a lake, clinging on to the rope and letting yourself slide down and down, and then clasping hands with someone on the lake bed for a brief moment before resurfacing once more. The time I spent this way always shone with a special brilliance for me.

*

Esaki was another of my matches. He did a tech job at a co-working space in Yokohama. I knew that was basically something like a shared office, but I was hazy on the details.

'About ten of us have been getting together recently to play these social deduction games. Do you know Werewolf?' Esaki asked me.

I told him I'd never heard of it.

'I'll invite you along next time we play – you should come and join us! The others are all great, too.'

And so a few days later, I found myself setting out for this mysterious co-working facility about ten minutes' walk from Yokohama Station. When I arrived, Esaki introduced me to everyone.

'This is Nanako, we met on PerfectStrangers. She looks for the perfect book to recommend to everyone she meets – she's a big hit on the site!' he was nice enough to say. It surprised me how casually he told his friends from outside PerfectStrangers that we'd met on a people-matching site, and I was flattered he'd said I was popular.

But what came as more of a revelation was that the people at the co-working space all knew PerfectStrangers, and didn't seem to think there was anything odd about it at all; in fact, they said things like, 'That's cool! I'm registered too, but I haven't actually met anyone yet,' and 'Oh yeah, I'm on there quite a lot. Maybe you could recommend a book for me sometime!' I'd never told my work friends about the matching site, or about what I was doing on it, because I was sure they'd think it was weird. But maybe here, that kind of thing was considered normal. I didn't know if this attitude was something peculiar to people who used co-working spaces, or people who worked in tech, or what.

That day, they taught me how to play Werewolf, the game Esaki had mentioned. It was a riot. I couldn't get enough of it, and after that I often took myself along to the co-working space.

Everything I saw and learned there was new to me. All the members brought in their own computers – wafer-thin MacBooks, naturally – and freelanced away. They all seemed to be developing and releasing apps, and were constantly saying things like, 'That reminds me, I made this app yesterday . . .' as nonchalantly as anyone else would say, 'Oh yeah, I went shopping at IKEA earlier.' I had no idea you could make apps that easily.

I only had a vague notion of what it meant to work in tech, but as I spent time with the co-working bunch, it started to become clearer. While it was still a bit nebulous, I could see it wasn't quite what I had imagined.

I'd always pictured tech work as being very current and trendy. It must be profitable, because the demand and the market were growing so rapidly, and it was like the job of the future – you could work at a café or even from home! But I'd never considered there might be a hierarchy within all that. And I'd assumed the prospects must be bright compared to the world of print books, where every day someone or other seemed to be gloomily predicting the industry's imminent demise.

In fact, with so many new hopefuls flooding into the tech sector, the people I met at the co-working space were having to struggle hard to establish themselves and create a source of stable income, and it didn't actually look like their future was much brighter than it was for us booksellers.

'Programming languages change all the time,' one of the co-workers told me. 'You can learn the ones that are in use now, but they'll basically be gone in a few years. You'll need to master the next generation of languages, or your job'll be taken by someone younger who learns faster.'

'I made this game recently that did really well and brought in quite a lot,' said someone else. 'Which *sounds* pretty sweet. But it took about half a year to develop. It used to be you'd work for a game company, and if you did well they might put you on the next big job. But nowadays, one hit isn't enough to get people interested in your next project. There's just not enough guarantee that it'll do as well as the first. Small developers like us can make money right now because app games are only just taking off, but once the big players join the party, we're done.'

When I'd first met this crowd, they seemed so cool, so free and easy. But in reality, no one anywhere was just cruising effortlessly and stylishly through life. Still – I was impressed by the way they at least had their hands on the wheel.

From then on, my circle of friends and acquaintances expanded rapidly, starting with those I'd met at the co-working space. It was partly thanks to the Werewolf game they'd taught me, which didn't work unless you had at least ten people or so. Game nights were springing up here and there and bodies were required; it didn't matter if the hosts knew you or not, you'd do just fine. This suited my own needs and my guiding principle, which was 'anything goes'. My mission was to explore new worlds and say yes to everything.

Other people noticed that I always came along to things on my own, so when I got to know them better, they'd invite me out for drinks or let me know when they had a spare ticket to a show, a gig, an event. And then the new people I met at *those* gatherings would ask me to more events, study groups, parties . . . and so a pattern was established and the number of people I met grew exponentially. More and more often, I found I wasn't exactly sure what the people I was hanging around with actually did for a living. Sometimes I didn't even know their real names.

Now I found it was a piece of cake to go to this and that event, and work my way into groups of unfamiliar people. If I went along to a gathering where I didn't know anyone, I could always hunt around for somebody who looked approachable. But if that didn't work, all I had to do was conspicuously stand on my own, *not* fiddling with my phone, and look as though I was at a loose end. A lot of the time, someone would come over and bring me into the fold. Just like on PerfectStrangers, you were only strangers for a moment. After that, you could chat merrily away to everyone as though you'd known them for yonks.

At first, I was a bit nervous if I was in a big crowd and didn't successfully manage to integrate, or if I couldn't keep up with the group banter, and I dreaded those situations. But it was never going to be possible to be comfortable at every get-together: not as comfortable as the people who already knew each other or who'd been there before. And when I just put my hands up and accepted this, accepted there would be plenty of disappointments, I stopped being scared that I wouldn't be able to keep up with everyone else. When I gave up trying to force myself to fit in and decided to only laugh when I genuinely felt like it, things became easier. Little by little, I worked out what to do with myself in those situations.

*

Now I was really, truly enjoying myself, just as I had once so desperately hoped I might.

But sometimes I'd find myself thinking about the situation with my estranged husband, and my spirits would sink. These thoughts blotted my heart like dark stains and snuffed out the lively music playing in my head. So to maintain the shine on my world, I had to cram in as much fun and excitement as I could, more and more and more. I kept the good times rolling and rolling, as though I was painting over those dark stains layer by layer. Even when it seemed as if there was no hope, as if my marriage problems were going to drag me back down again, I'd use one of these new worlds I'd discovered to pull myself into yet *another* new world, gaining strength from the after-images of a me that was feeling cheerful, doing fine.

Even I could see that I was just running away by seeking out fun and nothing else, that I was refusing to confront what needed to be confronted.

But how could I go on living if I didn't have some form of escape?

CHAPTER 5

UNSOLICITED ADVICE (AMONG OTHER THINGS)

Of course, not every encounter I had was a pleasant one. You couldn't hope to understand every single person you met, after all, and there was probably no such thing as perfect communication.

On one particular day off, I decided to list a chat as I was going shopping in Shinjuku. It was early afternoon on a week day – not the most convenient time for most people – and I only received one response, from a man called Konno. It looked like he'd just joined the site; there wasn't a single comment from anyone who'd met him. His profile read, 'My hobby is writing, and I have a novel in progress. My work is available on Kindle.' I felt a certain amount of trepidation, but I thought we might be able to talk books, so I decided to go for it.

The man who turned up at the café wore a rumpled old sweatshirt and joggers and had long, greasy black hair. He had a gloomy air about him.

'It's g-great to be able to talk to a g-girl like you,' he said with a gulping laugh.

Ooh, I haven't met anyone like him yet, I thought. I made an attempt at conversation, but his replies were so quiet I could barely hear him – I could only just make out that odd chuckle of his. It didn't seem like he was going to bring up any particular topics of his own, but when I mentioned e-books, he got out his iPad to show me what he'd written. It was a short story of about four pages, the genre perhaps best described as a mashup between sci-fi and historical fiction – the Warring States Period, to be precise. I did my best to get through it there and then in the hope it might give us something to talk about, but it was so incoherent I could make neither head nor tail of it. It was priced at a mere hundred yen on Kindle.

'Is it selling well?' I asked.

'No, not at all . . . What should I do? Do you have any ideas, maybe, about what I should change?' Konno asked. Perhaps he felt a little more comfortable now, because his voice was finally loud enough to make out.

'Um . . .' I faltered. For once, I found myself guiltily wishing that the thirty minutes would hurry up and be over. On the plus side, though, it made me realise that I'd never felt that way with any of my other matches.

Another occasion that frustrated me was when I turned up at the appointed café to find four people waiting. The person I'd actually arranged to meet was Yoshiki, but apparently the others were all on PerfectStrangers too, which was how they'd met. They were good friends and in regular communication, and when Yoshiki matched with me on the site, someone had floated the idea of them all coming along. Yoshiki said they were going out for drinks afterwards.

'Sorry about these guys, Nanako! But you're really popular, and everyone wanted to meet you – they all want you to recommend them a book.'

It was true that, thanks to my improved profile and my diligent efforts to pick books for people, I was rapidly climbing up the PerfectStrangers popularity ranking, and was sometimes up there in the top ten with the well-known entrepreneurs and long-time site users. I was delighted about that, but I didn't like being treated this way. For me, the real thrill and enjoyment of PerfectStrangers lay in the fact that the meetings were one on one. And more to the point – if you were going to let other people tag along, you could at least have the manners to send a quick message in advance and check it was okay.

It looked like the four friends had been at the café for some time. There were empty plates and glasses on the table.

'Hey, Nanako, if you haven't had dinner yet, you should get something! We've already eaten, but go ahead and order if you like. The burgers here are pretty good!' Yoshiki said. He was acting as though I was just someone who had showed up late to a party.

We had a crack at conversation, but trying to talk in a group just meant the chat had no direction. Besides, the others were already firm friends, so while they all started off by showering me with questions, they soon moved on to chatting away happily between themselves.

'I want a book recommendation too!'

'Why don't you just stick to CoroCoro Comic? Isn't that more your level?'

'Hey, come on, I'm not a kid!' and so on and so on.

You lot are managing just fine on your own, I thought, with rising irritation.

I decided not to hang around. When thirty minutes were more or less up, I drank the last of my iced tea, put my phone away in my bag and tried to signal that I was leaving.

'Oh, wait – let's get a photo together!' Yoshiki said. 'Excuse me!' he called loudly to a member of the café staff.

'Um – a photo?' I said.

'Yeah, like a souvenir! You know, I think PerfectStrangers is incredible – you can make so many new friends. And it was awesome we got to meet you today, Nanako! I'll invite you next time we all go out for drinks! Are you sure you can't stay any longer? Just another half hour?'

'Sorry, I have to go . . .' I said. 'I think PerfectStrangers is amazing too, though. But I'm not really that keen on being in photos, I'm afraid. Anyway, I'm going to head off now – enjoy the rest of your evening, everyone!'

I stood up, got out the money for my drink and left it on the table. Then, ignoring the cries of, 'Oh, what, are you going? What about the photo . . .?' I swiftly exited the café. I wasn't interested in being dragged into a situation where I had to pretend to be all chummy with everyone. *We could have been friends, if I'd met you all one at a time*, I thought.

It was also hard to have a good time with people who wouldn't really open up about themselves.

Ryoko was a philosophy student whom I'd arranged to meet in a café on Omotesando Avenue. After I'd arrived, she sent me a string of messages: 'Running a bit late,' 'I'm nearly there' and so on, before eventually turning up thirty-five minutes after the appointed time.

'Sorry about that,' she said.

'That's okay! I was a bit worried, though – did you have trouble finding this place? You should have said, I'd have come and met you,' I said, proffering a smile. I had slight misgivings about her attitude, though: she didn't seem particularly apologetic, and she just began to peruse the menu, without even smiling back. Still, I supposed if we could at least enjoy a good chat in the time we had left, that would be fine.

'You're at uni, aren't you?' I said, by way of breaking the ice. 'I saw you're studying philosophy. What kind of thing does that cover, exactly?'

'Well, I'm in my first year, so I've only just started. It's a kind of general course,' Ryoko said.

'It hasn't really got interesting yet, then? Have you always been into philosophy?'

'Um, yeah, I guess . . .'

'So how are you finding PerfectStrangers, anyway? What made you decide to sign up?' I asked, changing tack.

'I just kind of joined.'

'Oh, right. Well, how are you getting on with it? Do you like it?'

'I'm not really sure yet . . .'

And things continued in this way. Ryoko seemed to have no desire to expand on any of her answers, and she didn't ask me anything or offer up any other topics of conversation. It got tiring having to continuously think of something to say, and I wondered why she had bothered coming.

Of course, I was under no obligation to be the one to keep the conversation moving and come up with things to talk about. But if the chat never really got going and the thirty minutes passed without me being able to draw out what was really interesting about my match, it was my time that would have been wasted. On the occasions when the talk only covered safe topics, and I hadn't been able to open up personally or get to the heart of my match, I was left with a sense of regret. It did happen sometimes: I might not manage to get anywhere with someone, and the meeting would end without anything particularly noteworthy having occurred.

In these short encounters, the key thing was being able to press the other person with the right questions and coax them into revealing the things I wanted to know. The downside of learning this skill was that the back-and-forth became so quick and incisive, like a duel fought with two finely honed blades, that it made the banal small talk at work seem deadly dull afterwards.

So, not every exchange was a winner. But the one that taxed me most in the course of my career on PerfectStrangers, the one that took things to another level altogether, was my experience with Fujisawa.

*

Fujisawa was slightly older than me; he lived in Sendai and used PerfectStrangers on his occasional business trips to Tokyo. He told me that on the day of our meeting he would be in Tokyo for work, but he was planning to spend the following day wandering about the city before heading back up north, so he was happy to come out to Yokohama and meet up late in the evening.

After we'd arranged to meet, I suddenly remembered that a local cinema in Yokohama was doing a late-night showing of a film I really wanted to see, for one night only. I would have felt bad cancelling on Fujisawa, but I didn't want to miss the film either, so I invited him to come along, if he was interested. Fortunately he readily agreed, and we watched the film together and then went for a light supper and drinks. The trains had long stopped running for the day, but I could easily get a taxi home, so I wasn't worried. We walked the streets of night-time Yokohama, me playing tour guide to Fujisawa.

He'd said he was here for work, so I had assumed he must be staying in a hotel somewhere nearby. But when I asked him about this, he told me he planned to just hire a booth in an internet café or something and spend the night there. Yokohama didn't actually have that many internet cafés, though, and it was the weekend now, so I was worried none of them would have any booths free. Fujisawa tried calling a few different places to check. When he got off the phone, he said in a low voice that it looked like everywhere was full. He didn't seem familiar with the area, so I looked up the cheap lodgings in Ishikawacho that I'd used back in my homeless days to see if they had any space, and then I put Fujisawa in a taxi and gave him the address. I got myself another taxi and went home.

Fujisawa had said he'd actually just got back from holiday a few days before we met; he'd been off for a week or so on annual leave, backpacking around India. He'd told me with excitement about his impressions while he was there, and about his fascination with travel. So a day or two later, I sent him a message recommending the book *Midnight Express* by Kotaro Sawaki.

Midnight Express is a legendary travelogue set in the 1970s, and it still has its legions of devotees among backpackers today. There's something very pleasant about the way the author keeps an open mind and never lets anything get to him. And, pioneer of the genre that it is, the book conveys the joys of travel in a more real way than any other travelogue. It's so gripping that you'll be desperate to find out what happens next, and won't be able to put it down.

Fujisawa had told me he'd wanted to try and see India with an open mind, without any preconceived ideas, and I knew he was now considering where to go next. I thought *Midnight Express* would be a perfect fit.

Some time later, I received an encouraging reply. 'I'd actually come across the book before but never got round to picking it up. So you inspired me to finally give it a go, even though I was a bit sceptical about it (sorry!). But it was such a fascinating read! I ended up powering through all six volumes. It really reminded me of just how amazing it is to travel.'

And then that was that, and we never had any further communication with each other.

That is, until one day, I received an email out of the blue.

'How are you?' was the subject line. 'There was something really special for me about the night we spent together in Yokohama. So I wanted to write something about it. It's long and I kind of wrote it for myself, so it's sort of embarrassing, but I know you read a lot of books, so I wondered whether I could have your thoughts on it as a piece of writing? Your critique, maybe?'

For some reason, I felt a sense of foreboding. But I could hardly say, 'Nope, sorry, you're giving me the heebie-jeebies.'

My reflex was to hide my misgivings with a casual reply: 'Oh, sounds interesting. I don't know that I'll really be able to say anything very helpful, but I can read it if you like,' I sent.

What Fujisawa sent me was a porn novel, a monumental work weighing in at ninety pages of Word document, that began the night we met with me getting into his taxi, throwing myself at him and telling him, 'I'm lonely. I don't want to go home.' The more I read, the sicker I felt. The lengthy, explicit depictions of sex were bad enough, but it was scenes like the one of me raptly stroking Fujisawa's legs and admiring how lovely and smooth they were that really scarred me. I wondered whether, if I just kept reading, the thing would exhibit some interest as a novel. And clutching on to this faint, inexplicable hope – or maybe it was just morbid curiosity – I read through to the final page, struggling to breathe. But by the denouement I had become pregnant with Fujisawa's child and was giving birth to it as a single mother. Fujisawa had decided to leave me, though it made his heart ache, and go back to his family, in what you could safely call an incredibly outdated conclusion for a story purportedly set in the twenty-first century. And the writing had no particular literary merit after all, and had only served to make me feel queasy.

Anger, disgust, hopelessness, all welled up inside me. *Why did this have to happen to me when all I did was recommend him a book?* I thought, and *Why did he think it was okay to send this to me?* The questions swirled round and round miserably in my head.

Had I done something wrong? Had we had some conversation, had I said something that led him to the unavoidable conclusion that I had feelings for him? Should I have made it clearer that I didn't? But when exactly, at what point in the evening?

I realised I was pointing the finger at myself, searching myself for some fault. It was as though I was watching it happen to someone else; it sunk in properly then that people really do end up blaming themselves when they experience things like this.

You were entirely at liberty to have feelings for a person, and to see them as an object of sexual attraction. But surely *telling* them about it was a completely different matter. What was I supposed to think, reading this? Was I supposed to play along conveniently like the version of me in his pages? Reply with 'Ooh, I really enjoyed it, it got my pulse racing! ☆' Or did Fujisawa actually think I was going to start seriously assessing its merits as a piece of literature? Surely, surely he hadn't thought I'd be *pleased*?

No. He'd never had the tiniest shred of an idea about how it would make me feel. He hadn't given it a moment's thought. He had just written this thing because he wanted to write it, and sent it because he wanted to send it. If he'd done it maliciously, that would have been one thing, but this frightened me far, far more. This way, I didn't even figure as a person in his eyes.

Maybe he had thought it was fine. It wasn't rape, after all, he hadn't physically touched me, and if I didn't want to read it, well then, I could just stop. But he didn't seem to have considered that I might find it unpleasant for someone – someone I didn't even have feelings for – to write about me in this way, and then send it to me and tell me to read it.

It was partly because of the sexual aspect that the incident so thoroughly sapped my spirits. But more than that, I felt despair that there could have been such a gaping disconnect in our communication. We'd had an enjoyable evening together in Yokohama, we'd been communicating well and, at that point in time, I had felt like I trusted Fujisawa.

I was totally, utterly unequal to the task of replying and explaining how I felt. I quietly closed my email, turned off my computer and slumped face down on my futon.

Maybe it was time to call it a day with PerfectStrangers.

*

Looking back, I had by then met and recommended books to around fifty people on the site. I'd had plenty of successful encounters, but it was possible that, even among the people I'd met and parted with without incident, there were some who'd thought they would just respond to my listing and feign an interest in books if it meant they got to meet a woman, and who had no plans to actually read the book I recommended. That was certainly the feeling I'd got with my first two matches. When I considered this, suddenly it all seemed awfully pointless.

However, I soon pushed that thought out of my head. No – it didn't mean my efforts had all been in vain. So what if my matches had had ulterior motives? Did that give me the right to complain about it as though I were some kind of victim? On PerfectStrangers, you were free to meet people in whatever way you wanted – were people not allowed to hope that something might happen between a man and a woman? *Not* that it justified sending anyone an unsolicited porn novel, of course. But then, no one else had done anything like that.

Besides, I was making use of the site for my own purposes, too. Every time I met someone, I would rack my brain to find the right book for them. And since I'd gone to the trouble, I wanted them to take an interest; I'd be even more delighted if they went away and read whatever I'd picked. But I realised it had been my choice to take things so seriously. I could hardly complain if other people weren't that into the idea.

Books, books, books . . . What was it with me and books, anyway? Was I some sort of literary goodwill ambassador, or something? Once I started asking myself what it was I was actually trying to do, none of it really seemed to matter anymore. I let out a deep sigh.

Anyway – if I was going to keep at it getting experience of recommending books to people, I had to stop getting so indignant when people didn't seem to fully appreciate my painstaking efforts. If the book thing just provided an opportunity for people to get interested in me, that was enough. My matches didn't have to take me up on my recommendations; I should just be grateful to them for providing me with a chance to practise. That was all it was: nothing more, nothing less.

*

My husband and I were still meeting up to talk about our next steps, but dark clouds were gathering over the discussions. It increasingly felt as though we were on completely different pages. We still ate together once a month, but often now we found ourselves sitting there at an impasse.

On one particular occasion, we had finished our meaningless small talk and started attempting to address the elephant in the room when my emotions got the better of me.

'Why is it all about you?' I found myself saying, sharply. 'Have you ever tried thinking about how I feel?'

I'd spoken more forcefully than I'd meant to. My husband cast his eyes down as though in admission, and the conversation ground to a halt.

But my words pierced my own chest with the same force. Had I really considered how *he* was feeling? Enough that I could justify saying something so self-important? No – on the contrary, I'd been trying to avoid thinking about him at all. I wondered whether I had really been in a position to criticise Fujisawa, after all. To think I'd spent all this time with my husband, only to find I occupied no space inside him, nor he inside me.

And if that was us, and we were supposed to be a married couple, then who *could* you ever really build a proper relationship with? How did other people manage it?

*

Gradually, I found myself on PerfectStrangers less and less. It wasn't really down to the shock of the incident with Fujisawa, or anything like that. The cause lay somewhere else.

At first, PerfectStrangers had been like *Close Encounters of the Third Kind*, a succession of surprises and nervous thrills, where everything that appeared before me was fresh and new. Each person I met was totally different from the last, and they all had genuinely fascinating stories to tell. Even when the conversation never really took off, I always came away with something to think about, and I never felt bored. But I'd gradually got acclimatised to meeting strangers and recommending books, and at some point it had started to feel like I was just doing the same thing over and over again. It was fun watching the number of people I'd met climb higher, and I did vaguely wonder whether I should try for a hundred, but pushing onwards just to achieve a record didn't seem quite right.

Besides, I was busy on most of my days off now, catching up with people I'd met on PerfectStrangers and all the friends and acquaintances I'd found through connections made at the co-working space. Plus, I had finally got my act together and started looking for a new job.

Having said that, none of the ads on the job sites were very inspiring. My experience on PerfectStrangers had reaffirmed my love for books, and my desire to do some kind of book-related work had grown stronger. I couldn't find a single mid-career recruitment ad for any of the bookshop chains, however, and publishers only wanted people with experience for the sales and editing jobs on offer. Based on my work history, the only vacancies that showed up for me were management positions in chain restaurants, automatically selected because I'd ticked 'shop manager' for my current position. But I couldn't summon up an interest in a job that had nothing to do with books.

*

Endo and I had stayed friends after meeting through Perfect-Strangers. We went for coffee now and again, and on my days off I sometimes met him for a meal in Shibuya or Harajuku.

When we'd met that first time, I'd wondered if our friendship would develop into something more, but our sporadic exchanges on LINE were devoid of anything suggestive. It was always just things like 'Let's meet up again' and 'What are you up to at the moment?' – and besides, Endo only ever sent one-line messages anyway. Still, it didn't seem as though he was avoiding me, and if I messaged to invite him out for food he'd generally send a (single-line) reply: 'Sounds great! When?'

I wasn't normally good at talking to other people about my worries, but for some reason I could come straight out and tell Endo whatever I was thinking.

'I do want to work in a bookshop, or in something related to books,' I said. 'But it's really not profitable right now. Even the big chains are going down like dominoes, never mind those little independent shops outside train stations. Books have a low unit price, for a start, and low profit margins, so you can't make any money. There aren't any jobs going in normal bookshops.'

'You want to work in a bookshop?' Endo pondered. 'I wouldn't know about that, I never really go to them. I sometimes buy books if I have to and there's no digital version available. But if I already know which one I want, I just get it on Amazon. Physical books get in the way. Even if I buy *Shonen Jump* or another magazine in a convenience store, I just leave it in the overhead rack on the train when I'm done with it. Are bookshops really necessary? What are they there for?'

'What are they there for? I wonder . . .'

'Does it have to be a job involving actual physical books?' Endo asked.

'No, an online thing would be okay too . . .' I said. 'Maybe a sort of online bookshop. I could introduce books on a blog or a website and include links to Amazon. Become an affiliate, I think it's called. I wonder if something like that would make more sense.'

'I'm not sure,' said Endo. 'I think with books you only get to keep about three per cent of the price or something, which probably wouldn't be enough. Commission from the sale of a thousand-yen book would be thirty yen. So to earn a decent salary, say three hundred thousand yen a month, you'd have to sell ten thousand books every month. That definitely wouldn't be easy. Maybe you'd be better having some kind of sideline. I wonder what . . . Erotica? Idol merch? Nah, not going to win any prizes for imagination there . . .'

That was what I liked about Endo: even when things didn't look very hopeful, he kept me cheerful and never let the discussion get too downbeat.

'Combine books with something else . . . yeah, maybe,' I said. 'A lot of new bookshops offer food and drink now, or sell other stuff too, or hold events. If I was just going to run the place on my own, maybe I could put a bar in there.'

'Yeah, why not? So then it's a question of your income and outgoings. The shop rent might be around two hundred thousand yen, and then the rent on your own place might be . . . say, sixty thousand yen, if you economised. If you had ten customers a day who each spent three thousand yen, your takings would be around thirty thousand yen per day, nine hundred thousand per month . . . So you'd end up with a balance of about six hundred thousand yen. But you're going to need some days off, too, so maybe it would be a bit less. And you might not be able to bring in thirty thousand yen a day right from the off. Then there's buying in the food, the drink, the books . . . I wonder if you'd end up with anything left over?

'I think if you were savvy about it, you could get your bookshop bar featured in magazines, build up a buzz around it. I feel like you're trying to attract book lovers, though, people who'll get interested after seeing the shop in a magazine – but they're not necessarily the customers who'll visit every day. Your business would be propped up by locals and people living within easy distance. And then the focus might be less on the books. And if you were only just making enough to scrape by, maybe it wouldn't be quite what you'd imagined . . . What do you think?'

This was where Endo's experience of self-employment came to the fore; he had managed to sketch out the whole picture in a way that made it very easy to understand, and it really helped broaden my perspective.

'Yeah, what you're saying all makes sense,' I said. 'Wonder what I should do, then . . .?'

'Anyway, I don't know much about bookshops, I don't even really know whether it's a good idea to have a shop in general. But I'm sure you can make it work!' said Endo, turning the full force of his smile on me.

'What? If you have no idea, then how can you say that?' I said.

'Well, you came up with a concept on PerfectStrangers and made it succeed, didn't you? You hadn't even used Facebook before, but you thought up your own idea for something that would be popular, and it really took off. And now people are getting interested when they look at other people's reviews of you, and you've got a high level of customer satisfaction. If you can make something like that happen by yourself, you'll be fine leaving your job – I'm sure everything will work out somehow!'

'Things only worked out well for me on PerfectStrangers because other people gave me advice and pointed me in the right direction,' I said.

'And that happens even more when you go it alone!' said Endo. 'Besides, even if other people have helped you, you're the one who's actually doing it, Nanako. Some things are more difficult when you're on your own compared to when you're an employee, true – but everyone helps each other out a lot, with money and things too.'

'Sure . . . But people on PerfectStrangers don't actually have to pay me, do they? I mean, *you* make videos, they have real market value,' I argued doggedly.

Endo grinned knowingly and said, 'You know, in every industry there are a bunch of people with questionable job titles like "consultant" or "advisor" who teach amateurs about things with not very much substance, and unis and companies pay them fifty thousand yen or a hundred thousand yen a pop. You've probably already met some of them on PerfectStrangers! I don't know if it's a thing in the bookshop industry, but if you became a something-or-other advisor, you could probably make decent money.'

I was flattered that Endo thought I'd be good at that sort of thing, but the idea gave me mixed feelings. It wouldn't exactly be something to be proud of.

'Ugh, no way. I don't want to turn into some greedy grown-up, making money from a job with no real meaning!' I exclaimed. I tried to make it sound jokey, embarrassed because it seemed like something a kid would say.

'What are your priorities for work, then?' Endo asked.

'Something with more . . . *heart*, I suppose.' Even as I said it, I laughed self-consciously.

'So be an advisor with heart!' said Endo. I didn't know whether he meant it as a joke or if that was his actual advice, but as we talked, I began to feel lighter and lighter. Staying in my present job wasn't the only option; I could clearly see that now.

For the time being, all I could do was systematically sound out everyone in publishing I'd met through working at Village Vanguard.

'I'm thinking of changing jobs, do you know anywhere that might be hiring?' I would say. And then so that my pitch didn't die on its feet, I'd follow up by mentioning PerfectStrangers, the second half of my set piece. 'In fact, I've been uninspired at work recently, so I'm doing this slightly weird thing where I use a dating site to introduce books to people . . .'

That tended to amuse whomever I was talking to – most people would laugh and ask if they'd heard me right – and I was relieved to find I could talk about it anywhere and with anyone. It got easier and easier to publicly share what I was doing on PerfectStrangers, and people were incredibly interested, far more so than I'd expected. The positive responses outweighed the negative hands down.

While most people reacted with laughter or surprise, they naturally tended to express some concern, too. Was I sure it was okay? Weren't there weirdoes on the site? I should be careful – there were some scary people out there. I could see where they were coming from, so I tended to answer breezily with, 'It's actually fine, but thanks!' as though it was just common sense.

However, there were a few vexing people who would staunchly refuse to let it go. They were almost always men, middle aged or older, and they almost always said the same thing, too. It would start with something like, 'Sending messages is one thing, but don't you think it's dangerous actually meeting strangers in person like that?'

'Well, we meet in public, in cafés and places, so nothing terrible's going to happen,' I would say.

'But what if someone followed you, or tried to find out where you live?'

'That would be frightening, yes . . . But you take that risk just going about your normal life, too.'

'Well, look, I'm sure people seem nice, but sometimes you just can't tell what they're thinking. Men have ulterior motives, you know. All men do! Don't you think you should be more careful?'

Even if I'd managed to maintain a friendly smile up until that point, when someone said something like that to me, I'd feel my expression darken. I suppose these men just thought they were doing me a favour: warning me, for my own benefit, about a danger they assumed I was unaware of – not considering how I might feel about it, and never imagining they might possibly be offending me. They thought they understood the world so much better than I did.

A lot of men probably did have ulterior motives. Some men went ahead and laid them out on the table from the off. And there were even those, like Tsuchiya and Koji, the first people I'd met on PerfectStrangers, who would probably say without compunction that if there was no prospect of sex, then there was no point meeting up with a woman in the first place. And yet even if certain people did feel like that on some level, you could still form a friendship or a relationship of trust with them based along different lines.

But to these people unused to meeting strangers, the idea of a rendezvous with an unknown woman was inextricably linked to the idea of sex, and they probably couldn't conceive that it might possibly be anything else. I wished I could show them the world I'd discovered through PerfectStrangers. Two people unknown to one another, even a man and woman, could meet one to one and experience so many other wonderful things. People really were capable of being kind to each other. In these past few months I'd seen it all first hand: the good and the bad.

If I told those men about the incident with Fujisawa, they'd probably assume they'd been right all along. 'See!' they might say with relish. 'That's exactly what I'm talking about.' But it was only because I'd accepted the risk of things like that happening that I'd had so many other interesting encounters.

I'm sure they did exist somewhere out there – the perils of dating sites, men with ulterior motives, as envisaged by these unimaginative people who got their ideas from the TV and the internet. But all my days of encountering strangers, all the ways in which they'd helped me, shone radiantly in my mind, and this misdirected advice from people who just didn't understand that didn't bother me in the slightest. Their words were as insignificant as dust on the wind.

Except for the exchanges with these tiresome old duffers, it would be fair to say that only good things came of me revealing my experiences on PerfectStrangers. I got a bit of a reputation for being an unusual bookseller, for starters, and this led to me receiving all sorts of invitations and being introduced to even more people. 'Hey, Nanako, I'm going out for drinks with a friend; she's a bookseller too, would you like to come? She's also really interesting – she organises her own book fairs in her shop and also makes this free zine. I think you'll get on really well!'

All this made me realise that if you just did things a little bit differently, it could lead to new encounters – even if you were still in the same old place you always had been. I'd dived into the world of PerfectStrangers to escape my own lacking life, a life that consisted solely of Village Vanguard and trips around bookshops. And yet when I'd given the door just a little push, I'd found another world right there on the other side, one that had seemed far away but had really been so close: the World of Booksellers. Stepping through the door, I found that here were all these people sparkling with individuality, putting serious thought into the question of how to sell books, living their lives with the same hopes and fears as me. *I've found my people!* I thought. *And they were here all along! Why didn't anybody tell me?*

A lot of the booksellers I met were on social media, which I'd been shying away from; they were using it to bridge the gap between different companies and form a network of peers. When

I followed suit, I found dozens of people doing wonderful jobs, and any number of people I could respect.

I had found one more door, one more new world.

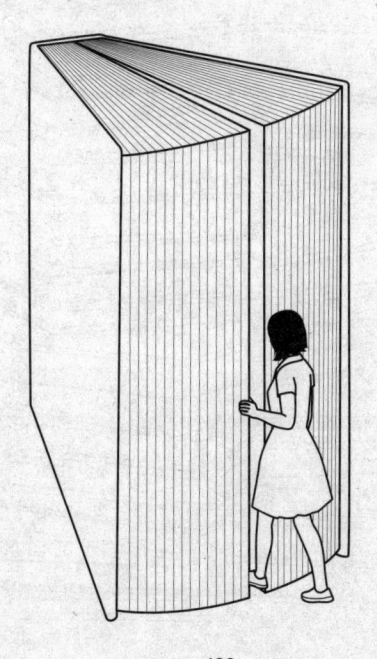

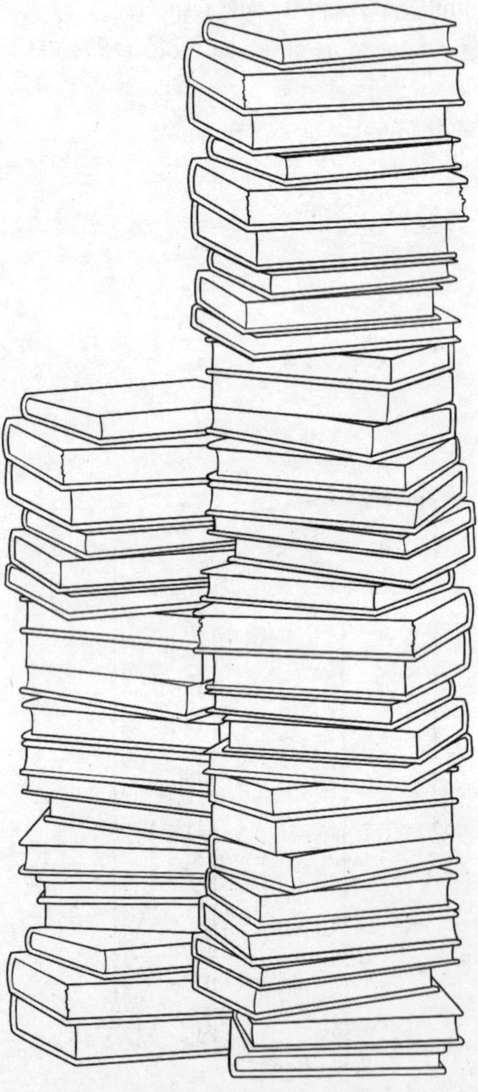

CHAPTER 6

FACING THE FINAL BOSS

By now I had faced a good fifty strangers in single combat (by which I mean chatted to them one on one, of course). The goal of my original quest, if you could call it that, had been to hone my skills in selecting books for people I didn't know, and I was certainly improving. However, I had also experienced another significant side effect: talking to strangers suddenly seemed a lot less daunting. In fact, it was now almost a walk in the park for me.

Around this time, I went on my first ever group date: four guys, four girls and a few rounds of drinks. It was a pleasant enough experience – I was impressed by the gentlemanly behaviour of our male company, and the beauty of the group-dating etiquette. But to be honest, I'd got so used to meeting people one on one now that I really felt like I was having to pull my punches. There was something so lukewarm about talking four on four. I couldn't bring myself to care about the 'Guess what clubs everyone did at uni!' quiz – I wanted to go deeper! I kept thinking what I'd ask each of the others if we were talking on our own, but I didn't want to upset the mellow mood, so I refrained from diverting the conversation. Instead, I just smiled as I listened to my companions, joined in every now and then with a mild quip, and came away having learned how to act on group dates.

After we parted, all smiles, at the south entrance to Shinjuku Station, and I was on my own again, I wondered whether it wouldn't be more productive to just flag down a likely looking passerby and see if they wanted to get a coffee or something. Of course, I understood why most people wouldn't want to. Anyone approached on the street like that would be suspicious. *Who is this person? Is she trying to get me to join some dodgy religious group? Or a pyramid scheme? Trying to pull some kind of scam? Is she a new kind of streetwalker? Or is she married – is she planning to come on to me and then blackmail me? Could she be a sex maniac? Or is she some other, different flavour of unsavoury . . . ?*

You'd have difficulty getting anyone to even stop and speak to you. And yet, despite knowing all that, I had lost my inhibitions to such an extent by now that I thought, *I bet if I just tried it, it would actually go pretty well.*

And so, for the first time in my life, I threw down the gauntlet to a man in a bid to get to know him better. The man in question was Kuroiwa, the organiser of a round-table event I happened to be attending. There were fifty or so attendees, and he was the one calmly running the show. He worked in tech but was fairly quiet, without that typical tech-bro energy, and I was impressed by the laid-back, gently humorous way he talked. He seemed to be a popular character, though, and my first impression was that he was well out of my league. I'd only ever come across his name before – he happened to be on PerfectStrangers too, and he sometimes listed meetings – so it was interesting to see him in person.

He might be out of my league, I thought, *but I bet it would be fun to be friends.*

The talk had ended and everyone was mingling, but Kuroiwa was constantly surrounded by people. I waited for my opening and then made my approach.

'This is my first time here, what a great crowd you managed to bring in!' I said.

'Hi! Well, thanks for coming,' said Kuroiwa.

'I'm on PerfectStrangers,' I told him. 'I heard about this event from someone I met through the site. You list meetings sometimes too, don't you? I always thought it would be nice to meet up, but the timing never worked out.'

'Oh yeah, I'm on PerfectStrangers, but I don't use it that often. So you're on there too? What's your username?' he asked.

'Nanako.'

'Okay, I'll look you up.'

'Actually, I do this thing where I recommend the perfect book for everyone I match with on the site,' I said.

'Oh, really? That's cool, I've never heard of anything like that before.'

I didn't know whether Kuroiwa's smile was genuine or whether he was just being polite, but at least he'd remember me.

After the event, we connected on Facebook and I looked at his timeline. Unrelated to his day job, he occasionally blogged on subjects like the trials and tribulations of prolonged male virginity. He wrote about these light-hearted topics in an entertaining, amusing way, and I found myself sighing and thinking that some people just had class, no matter what they did.

I scanned through more or less the whole blog and then sent Kuroiwa a long message with my thoughts. His writing was genuinely interesting, that was part of it – but mainly, I wanted to firm up our connection. His reply was positive.

'Thanks for taking the time to share your thoughts! I don't normally get the chance to get any serious feedback on my blog, because of the subject. You write really well – must be because you're a bookseller! I feel like I learned a lot from your writing, even though you were the one complimenting mine. By the way, I saw your PerfectStrangers page, you've met so many people! I'd really love a book recommendation from you if I get the chance sometime.'

Bingo! I composed my follow-up. 'I'm on a quest to improve my book-recommending skills right now, so I'd love to pick something for you! I saw you sometimes list meetings for Tuesdays at 2pm in Takadanobaba, but that's a bit tricky for me. Next week I'm off Wednesday and Friday, though, and I could meet you somewhere around Shibuya or Shinjuku. Daytime or evening, either is okay.' I'd intentionally invited him in a way that would make it easy for him to let me down gently if he wasn't actually interested.

He soon replied: 'Okay, what about Tuesday 6pm in Shinjuku? I don't have anything on that evening.' Yes! This was the perfect formula for potentially having dinner together.

And thus I learned the art of picking up men. Having said that, I wasn't creeping closer to Kuroiwa in pursuit of a relationship or sex – just proactively trying get to know someone whom I'd met and thought seemed nice. There was really nothing complicated about it.

Though we hadn't initially met through PerfectStrangers, the way our meeting had come about was still slightly unconventional, and I went along a little nervous, hoping we'd find things to talk about. But Kuroiwa was a great conversationalist, entertaining and good at keeping the chat going, and we moved from talking about his blog to discussing this idea of men's inexperience being linked to their power of imagination. That was a concept I was particularly interested in, and it helped shift the conversation up a gear. We started talking about Hikaru Ijuin and Jun Miura, who'd co-authored a book on male virginity, and then moved on to recent manga by Nayuka Miné and Shigeyuki Fukumitsu, and then *From Miyamoto to You*, arguably a landmark work of manga on the subject. Kuroiwa hadn't heard of Chokkaku Shibuya's manga *The Chronicle of the Woman Who Sings Bossa Nova*

Covers of Those J-pop Songs They Always Play in Cafés, so I heartily recommended it to him, and in return he regaled me with amusing titbits about the changing image of male virginity in the world of adult video, and various other things I had no idea about.

On the way out, Kuroiwa said breezily, 'Well, definitely let me know if you have any more recommendations!' It seemed like he'd enjoyed the evening. I certainly had.

I'd initially worried he would think I was odd, asking to meet up when I didn't really know him. But in the freelance business, perhaps that was standard fare. Or maybe it was just Kuroiwa's personality. Whatever it was, I felt reassured. It was as though he'd let me know that even if I ventured beyond the borders of PerfectStrangers, I could still make friends with people in the exact same way, if I wanted to – it was no big deal. And if I was allowed to apply the rules of PerfectStrangers to the outside world, well, there was no limit to the number of people who might want to hit that button and sign up for a chat with me.

Surfing on this wave of optimism, I sent a spontaneous message to Sakuma, a writer on a funny entertainment site and apparently a friend of Kuroiwa's. I looked at this particular site often and had clocked Sakuma as someone whose articles were always interesting – and then one day he popped up on my Facebook feed, having a merry exchange with Kuroiwa. Well, this wasn't my first rodeo. Without sparing a thought for the fact we'd never spoken before, I found myself very casually extending him an invitation to meet.

'Hi, I realise this is a bit of a random message, but I'm a big fan of your blog and just wanted to say hello. My day job is managing a Village Vanguard, but right now I'm also roaming the city improving my book-recommending skills – I use this site called PerfectStrangers to meet strangers and try and pick out the perfect book for them. I got talking with Kuroiwa recently, and then I got quite excited when I saw you come up on his Facebook, so I just had to message! I also really like the articles you write for that website – they're my favourite part of the site, actually, and . . .' I went on in this vein for a bit. '. . . Anyway, I was wondering if you'd like to go for coffee sometime? And this is very much optional of course, but if you tell me what kind of thing you like to read, I can recommend a book for you.'

Well, here we go, I thought. If he was wary of me, so be it. And he might be really busy, anyway. But even if he didn't reply, it would have been worth a shot.

I was resigned to the possibility that nothing would come of me reaching out like this. But it was almost as though my disheartenment had conveyed itself to Sakuma, because when his reply came back, it was encouraging.

'Thanks for your kind words!' it read. 'I'd love a book rec! I'm usually free Tues and Fri, around midday to evening, if I'm not out getting material for my writing. Whereabouts do you live?'

Things proceeded much more smoothly than I'd expected, and two days later I was meeting Sakuma in Saint Marc Café in Nakano. He wasn't on PerfectStrangers himself, so this was the moment I had completely broken away from the matching site. Now, the whole of the real world had come within range of my advances, and my party trick of suggesting the perfect book had well and truly evolved into a strategy for flirting. Was it really okay to use it for such an ignoble cause?

'That's cool – so you're like a wandering warrior who goes around recommending books to people. Have you met anyone interesting?' Sakuma asked.

'Hmm, well there was this one guy . . . A few months after I met him, he sent me an entire porn novel featuring me and him as the main characters,' I said.

'What? That's wild!'

I was a long-time enjoyer of Sakuma's blog and articles and I really admired him – he felt like someone from such a distant sphere that I couldn't quite believe I was talking so normally with him. Plus, although I'd felt truly awful when I received that novel from Fujisawa, now that time had passed I found I was able to joke about it, and it didn't seem like such a big deal after all. I was glad it had provided me with an amusing anecdote.

Which reminded me, I was still receiving periodic messages from Tsuchiya, my very first PerfectStrangers match.

'How've you been?'

'Have you found a boyfriend?'

'Long time no see! Want to go out for yakiniku?'

'Summer's here! Have you been busy?'

He kept sending them, just like a bot, even though he must be able to see I'd read them all and not replied to a single one.

'Oh yeah, and then there was this guy...' I said, showing Sakuma the Messenger screen, and he burst out laughing.

'Aww, he just doesn't give up hope! Even though they're all marked as read, and you've never replied! That's amazing,' he said. Now that my exchange with Tsuchiya had also come in handy as a source of amusement, I felt like his ghost had been laid to rest.

Sakuma's own writing was very interesting, so I was surprised to hear he hardly read any books himself.

'With print books, even essays and things . . . it's like they're so slow-moving, you know? I've got too used to the pace of reading online now, I find books hard to get through,' he said.

I wasn't really sure if it would be a good fit, but I recommended him Sekishiro and Naoki Matayoshi's co-authored collection of freestyle haiku, *I'm Only Here for the Deep-Fried Oysters*. It had a sort of out-there vibe, similar in tone to Sakuma's blog, but more importantly, there were no big chunks of text. Single lines were imbued with humour, or conveyed a sense of tragic determination in the face of adversity, like advertising slogans. I thought the book might help dispel Sakuma's feelings of ambivalence towards reading and give him a positive impression of the printed word.

*

It almost seemed to me that, if I could meet a series of strangers like this and get to know them so easily, all I had to do was keep going and soon I'd be able to make friends with anyone. It might be difficult with celebrities and writers, of course, anyone with lots of fans – but then it wasn't as though I was randomly looking to get chummy with idols and comedians and people. If I just had a proper reason for wanting to meet someone, then maybe there was nothing extraordinary about it. Maybe I could actually talk to almost anyone.

So, if I could talk to anybody, potentially get to know any person, then of all the people out there, who did I most want to meet? The question just playfully popped into my head, but the answer came back instantly. I wanted to meet Kenji Yamashita from Gaké Shobo, the bookshop I loved most in the world.

*

I first came across Gaké Shobo in my mid-twenties, when I was travelling alone in Kyoto.

I'd got on the city bus and ridden for ages and ages, passing through bustling tourist areas and out the other side, over to the eastern edge of the city. The bookshop sat there all alone in an entirely unremarkable location, with not a single sightseer strolling by. This description might bring to mind some kind of dignified, unassuming establishment – but not so. You could easily tell you'd reached the shop. Its high surrounding wall seemed to be made of a jumble of rough rocks (the word 'gaké' in the shop's name meant 'cliff', so maybe that had something to do with it). What was more, sticking out of this 'cliff' was the front half of a car – apparently the shop's emblem.

I had opened the door tentatively and ventured inside. The interior decor was based around dark wood, and the space was fairly dimly lit. Echoing through the shop were strains of an enigmatic acoustic tune with Japanese vocals, the likes of which I'd never heard anywhere else.

All over the place I glimpsed traces of the weird and wonderful books I loved so much. And yet in complete contrast to Village Vanguard, where I'd just started working at the time, they were arranged within the space with such a sense of elegance and calm, in a way that really impressed me. Intriguing publications I hadn't come across before – books from small presses, niche cultural magazines – were lined up in neat rows, and each gleamed enticingly. I was used to seeing all sorts of unusual books at Village Vanguard, but here, I was strongly drawn to every single book I encountered; it felt like there was something special about each volume I picked up. I was enthralled, as though I had fallen under a spell.

In my excitement, I went round and round the shop. In one corner was a chair and an acoustic guitar, with a sign saying, PLAY ME, which made me smile. And stuck up on the side of a bookshelf at the back of the shop was a piece of writing: 'What I did on my school trip – Kenji Yamashita, age 5'. I wondered whether it had been written by the owner. On first read it just seemed like a bog-standard child's story, the kind of thing any kid could write – but then I started to get the feeling that maybe it actually had some profound significance.

What had been the intention in sticking the writing up there? I couldn't really tell. But I sensed there was a wish to discombobulate people, a puckish spirit, coexisting with a feeling of quiet, of unexpected books lined up in unobtrusive rows. There were a few more little almost-invisible touches of madness sprinkled around the shop. I fell captive to the place and its distinctive charm.

I was reminded of something. Yes – the thrill I had felt when I was about nineteen, when I experienced Village Vanguard for the first time. Village Vanguard was loud and assertive, true. There, we piled up books we thought were great and plastered POP signs all over them until you could hardly even see the merchandise anymore. We took a very in-your-face approach to attracting customers. Maybe that was why it struck me now, seeing the merits of books being conveyed in a way that was so different. Something about the selection of titles, the way they were arranged, the chilled-out atmosphere . . . I didn't know what it was exactly, but all of it convinced me that Gaké Shobo had been put there for me. I felt like I could stay in there for hours and hours – and the longer I did spend there, the heavier grew the pile of books in my arms. I eventually ended up buying so many, you'd never have thought I was supposed to be travelling.

From that day onwards, I visited the bookshop again and again. Well – I say that, but Kyoto was a long way away, so the most I could manage was once or twice a year. No matter how many times I set foot in that shop, I was never bored or disappointed; in fact, my certainty about the place only grew firmer. Whenever I went back, there it was, perfectly matching that ideal image in my mind, exactly how it had been when I'd fallen so deeply in love with it. The atmosphere of the place restored the part of me that had been missing while I was away, and every time I'd visited since, I'd been able to reset myself. Gaké Shobo quickly became something akin to the core of my being. The feeling was one of adoration, almost like falling in love.

I wondered whether this emotional attachment might be just in my head. Before I found Village Vanguard, I'd hardly been to any bookshops. Maybe they were always like this; maybe other places would touch me just as deeply. To test this theory, I took myself along to an assortment of well-known independent bookshops in Tokyo and Kyoto. Every single one was lovely, I liked them all, and yet none of them stirred up that same fierce emotion in me, none of them drove me to distraction in the same way. So, I wasn't just imagining it: Gaké Shobo really was extremely special to me.

At some point, I was transferred within Village Vanguard and relocated to Kyoto. I spent a year and a half in the city, and I was absolutely over the moon about being able to go to the shop more often. Every visit, I discovered all sorts of books I'd never known existed. But it wasn't just that. I was sustained by the shop itself, by its very nature: by the way it always felt so unfailingly right, the way it occupied such a special place in my heart.

And yet, it had always been completely unthinkable that I might actually approach the shop's owner and tell them how much I liked the place. I was a worrier and an introvert by nature, and it had never even occurred to me that it might be nice to try and talk to them.

I did wonder what the owner was like. Was that him over there? Or could it be her? And then at some point, I came across a photo of him in a magazine interview.

Yamashita. So it's his shop . . .

I imprinted his picture on my mind, as though I were reading an article about a famous film director or a writer. That had been enough for me.

But now I'd asked myself, 'If you could meet anyone at all, who would you most want to meet?' And what was more, I'd already answered the question – and now suddenly I'd found myself standing face to face with the final boss. I mustered my resolve and decided to email Yamashita.

First I'd introduce myself, tell him I was an admirer of the shop and a long-time customer, and then say I had a request – that I knew it was sudden, but could we meet? It would be great if we could chat, just thirty minutes would be fine.

I'd tell him about the first time I visited Gaké Shobo, the impact it had on me, the fact I'd visited again and again and yet my affection for the place had never wavered. That I had this special affinity with the bookshop, an obsession that went beyond it merely being my favourite one . . .

The more I wrote, the more I felt my words were superficial, hackneyed, the kind of thing people said all the time. They were failing to capture the way I felt. I experienced bitter disappointment at how useless language was when it came to talking about the things you really loved.

There was something about the people I'd met so far, people like Kuroiwa and Sakuma: they weren't afraid of making stupid mistakes, or of facing rejection or defeat on the path to their goals. They made bold decisions, because they knew there was nothing to lose.

And yet Gaké Shobo was something I'd been tenderly carrying within me all this time, like my internal compass. If Yamashita recoiled from me in suspicion, if the shop and I became estranged, that would really hurt.

But my feelings had already carried me this far. I would never happen upon the chance to talk to Yamashita, not like with Kuroiwa, so as awkward as it was, sending a message out of the blue was the only method of approach I had. If he read it and thought I was just a regular customer and nothing more, that was fine. And if he thought I was out of my mind, so be it. I could only brace myself and accept that telling him my feelings like this might mean game over.

I wanted to settle the matter once and for all and not get into some protracted back and forth.

'I'm actually going to be in Kyoto next month, on the 20th and 21st,' I typed. 'If it's not a bother, would you be free at all on either of those days? I know this might be an inconvenience, so if you're busy, don't feel obliged to say yes, and don't worry about replying. Please just let me know if you think we might be able to meet.' And the email was done.

I didn't have any existing plans to visit Kyoto, of course. If he said yes, then all I had to do was go. I'd just thought if I didn't specify the date, it would end up being a case of, 'Sounds good, we should arrange something sometime,' and it might never actually happen. As for why I'd picked those dates – well, the trip would coincide with my birthday. Alarmingly, I appeared to have plotted to make meeting Yamashita a birthday present to myself . . .

Once I'd sent the email, I thought back over what I'd done. The very idea was enough to make me feel absolutely mortified. But the message was winging its way through the ether now, and there was no turning back.

And then one day a month later, at eight o'clock in the evening, there I was in Kyoto, meeting Yamashita.

Yamashita said he often came to this little bar. It was a comfortable place, pleasant but not pretentious, and the staff were sincere and friendly; it was like Gaké Shobo, in a way.

I was so nervous. My throat was dry, my jaw was paralysed, my tongue was stuck to the top of my mouth. If Yamashita asked me what I'd wanted to talk to him about, I would have to apologise and say that actually, there wasn't really anything in particular. But he was courteous, and he began chatting away normally as though it was only natural, as though we already had some kind of relationship where that made sense. I was beyond grateful.

'So, you've been working at Village Vanguard for a good while, then. And you spent time in Kyoto, didn't you? I think you said in your email. When was that?' he asked.

At first I fought the urge to run away and hide. I felt like some kind of repulsive, green, slimy monster sitting in front of Yamashita, and I was sure my forehead was about to break into a sweat. But as we talked, I gradually began to find my feet. Breathing got easier, and I came back to myself. And when I did, it turned out there were so many things I wanted to say, and to ask, and I felt like I could go on chatting with him forever.

As the mood relaxed, he shared candid, sometimes unexpected opinions – 'Does that book sell well at Village Vanguard? It's a big seller here, but I actually thought it was awful!' – as well as anecdotes about his childhood, about his time as an editor of erotica, about how he started Gaké Shobo. I let myself go and laughed at his stories.

I'd just been to the loo and was washing my hands when I saw my own familiar face staring back at me in the mirror. It wasn't delight I felt at that moment, so much as a sense of wonder. It was as though I'd locked eyes with some mysterious creature, as though I'd found myself in some distant, alien land.

Yamashita talked unstintingly to me about all sorts of things: the recent fad for amateurish books extolling the virtues of simple living; highly curated 'boutique bookshops'; his shop's own selection of titles . . . I told him I really liked the books he'd chosen, and the space he'd created.

'Well, I didn't choose the books for me. They're not ones that suit my tastes, they're ones that suit the customers,' he said, before sharing some more of his thoughts about the relationship between a shop and its clientele.

'But still, people come here and want to buy the books because they think you've chosen them, don't they?' I said. I knew what he was getting at, but even so, the shop was Yamashita through and through. There was so much I hadn't asked him yet. I still couldn't believe I was allowed to discuss things with him like this, like an equal.

Time flew by and soon it was eleven, and the bar was closing. We were the only two people left. And yet even then, Yamashita was nice enough not to suggest heading off. I was so loath to lose a single moment of my time with him, I couldn't bring myself to mention it either.

He sat there without moving a muscle, almost as though he was determined not to leave. He was like a kindly father, listening patiently on and on to the witterings of a small child: 'Um, and then, and then, another thing . . .'

Yamashita said he'd gone home after leaving the shop and then come out to the bar on his bicycle. The place I was staying was on his way home, so he walked me back, pushing his bike.

I thanked him as we stood in front of my lodgings, and then we parted and I watched him get smaller and smaller as he cycled away.

That night I lay in bed, gazing up at the ceiling and mulling over my feelings. There was no chance I'd be able to sleep any time soon. A wave of euphoria was washing over me now, as though it had been delayed somewhere along the way; it made me want to scream and shout, and I realised I was gripping the duvet fiercely. *So incredible things like this really do happen.*

And just like when a single answer in a crossword puzzle leads you on to the next, and then the next, and then all the rest, this one quiet evening had given my soul its bearings.

Now that the puzzle had been solved, I understood. Those all-pervasive topics, those questions I'd felt were being forced on me – 'Is it better to be single or married?' 'Which should you prioritise, work or home?' 'Should you have children or not?' – they had never been the right questions in the first place; they didn't pinpoint what was really important in my life. When I was forced to confront questions like those, I always felt like I was losing sight of the lines that defined who I was. I'd thought it was my fault I couldn't come up with any proper answers, and I'd felt so useless. But tonight, right now, I could see my own outlines clear and bright, sparking and fizzing as though coursing with electricity.

I didn't need ordinary happiness. I didn't need romance, or marriage. I didn't need money or stability. I didn't need anything.

All I needed was to live my life, and keep believing in the hope I'd seen today.

I could see it clearly now: the happiness I'd been searching for. That was the kind of night it was.

CHAPTER 7

SORRY, GRANDPA

The seasons were changing, autumn turning to winter.

Down a cul-de-sac, in a residential area that was so quiet you'd hardly think it was just ten minutes' walk from Yokohama Station, was a perfectly ordinary two-storey house. It wasn't one of those elegantly renovated traditional homes that are so on trend at the moment. Just a building of the most unlovely type; going there felt like visiting your grandparents' house. This was Café Hesomagari – 'Café Contrarian'.

I was still hanging out at the co-working space fairly regularly, and it was there I met the café's owner one day. In the course of our conversation, it transpired he'd also worked as a manager at Village Vanguard, of all places, and since our first encounter I had been visiting his café from time to time.

Café Hesomagari was another one-of-a-kind dreamland. Spending time there felt different from chilling out with the laid-back tech workers I'd met through PerfectStrangers, or chatting with the friendly booksellers. The café's main room had a tatami mat floor laid out with old, threadbare cushions to sit on, and around the walls were bookshelves crammed with manga. Most of the books looked as though they'd been stewing in soy sauce, the pages were so yellow. They had handwritten POP signs stuck on them, too, each of which piqued my interest, and on occasion I was delighted to come across older comics that I'd been wanting to read for a while.

Here you were free to absorb yourself in the manga, do some old-school gaming on the Famicom, get slowly inebriated until you were slumped on the floor, or just chat to the owner and the other customers. If I happened to drop by without checking what was going on, I would often find a live performance in progress, with someone singing and playing guitar. The café's customers were generally hard up and unable to fit in to society, and they all loved the old books and the quiet murmur of the music.

It was like heaven to me, this comforting café. There was something affirmative about the space: as though here, social dropouts were acknowledged and accepted just as they were. It was a lot like Village Vanguard, back when I first joined.

'I'm thinking of doing a sort of event here. D'you want to take part?' the café's owner asked me one day. 'I can't find anything I want to read lately, so I thought maybe everyone could recommend me some books I might like. Whoever's book interests me most, wins. Basically an event by me, for me – but there you go.'

'That sounds great! I'd love to take part!' I said.

SORRY, GRANDPA

I was to be one of four contestants: the others were Tweed, who ran a vintage bookshop in Hakuraku, a few stations away; Sonton, who worked in a bookshop and was also publishing a literary zine; and Shinji, who was lodging for free upstairs in Café Hesomagari at the time.

The format was like a loose version of Bibliobattle – basically a sort of book slam. On the day, some of the café's regulars also turned up to watch. I had decided to stake everything on two books I'd been keeping up my sleeve for just such an occasion.

'My first book is *Sightseeing*, by Rattawut Lapcharoensap, a Thai-American author,' I began.

My chosen book was wonderful in itself, of course, but there were a few other reasons I thought this one worked well as a recommendation. Firstly, there was the novelty of it being set in Thailand, and then there was the fact that the author had gone AWOL for a while after writing it. All this made it easier to get people to take a lively interest.

'It's a collection of truly beautiful short stories set in Thailand,' I continued. 'It paints a vibrant picture of the daily lives of people living in poverty. A lot of the stories are sad, but the vivid portrayal of these characters who're doing their best to live for the moment is something that will really stay with you, and give you fresh hope. *Sightseeing* is still not all that well known over here, but foreign-literature enthusiasts are already praising it highly. And I know some people aren't keen on the style of language in translated books, but this one reads really smoothly.'

I was happy to see that everyone was passing round my copy of the book and flipping through the pages with interest.

'Huh, I've never heard of this one.'

'Looks fascinating!'

As the spectators perused the book, I decided to make the most of the nice momentum I'd built up. 'I especially like the story called "At the Café Lovely",' I carried on. 'These two teenage brothers go to a brothel for the first time, but the younger boy gets frightened and starts yelling and crying, so the older brother has to leave before he's finished, and in the end the two of them get on their motorbike and speed off home. It's just got this real heart-rending sadness and beauty to it. Oh – and the last story, "Cockfighter", that's also really fantastic.' I had ended up giving too much away, but I just couldn't help it.

Then it was time for my second book. This one was different from *Sightseeing* in that it wouldn't suit everyone, but I thought it would pass muster with the café customers.

'Now, I think this one is a masterpiece, although admittedly a bizarre, offbeat one. It's *Youth and Perversity*, by contemporary artist Makoto Aida,' I said. 'It depicts the events of a high-school ski trip, told through the protagonist's diary. The author includes all these details that seem designed to make you wonder whether he's actually writing about his own teenage years. However, the contents of this journal would blow any budding romance to pieces, because they detail our narrator's predilection for the scatological, I guess you could say – by which I mean, his desire to peep at the object of his affections while she's defecating.

'Now, personally, that's not something I'm into. In fact, I found it pretty gross, and I almost wanted to put the book down. And yet, there was just something lively and engaging about the story that kept me reading – and it turned out to be a really, truly entertaining story. There's an unexpected twist in the final scene, like you get in a thriller, and the whole thing affected me in a way that's hard to describe, but it was a feeling you just don't get with normal books. Makoto Aida once held a solo art exhibition called "Sorry For Being a Genius", and it's true: his book is so unique and entertaining, it really *can* only be described as genius!'

It looked as though Café Hesomagari's owner had taken a real interest in the book after hearing my pitch, which was very gratifying.

Then it was the turn of the other participants to enthusiastically showcase the books they thought would be perfect for the owner's next read. Poetry collections like Hiroyuki Sasai's *Eternally from My Mouth*; Craft Ebbing & Co.'s *Cloud Collector*, with its depictions of an enigmatic imaginary world; philosophy books like *Laozi and the Boy*; religious tomes like *Conversations with God* – an eclectic selection of titles was put forward, and I enjoyed hearing about them all. Each contestant made an impassioned case for their choices, and I was won over every time. I'm not just saying this, but I'd have happily picked up any of the books straight away, and it looked as though our audience felt the same.

To my great delight, in the end the café owner selected my entry, *Youth and Perversity*, for the book-I-most-want-to-read grand prize. This more or less marked the end of the event, but after that I sat in a circle with the others and we chatted for a while.

'That was actually really great! Who'd have thought it was so interesting hearing other people's recommendations?' said Tweed.

'Yeah. I'd quite like to try it again sometime,' said Sonton.

'Why not?' I said. 'We could do an event like today, but where we call in customers one by one, find out about their reading habits and their problems and whatever, and then all join forces and fire away with our recommendations.'

My fellow contestants approved of this idea.

'Could we make that work? It sounds great!' said Sonton.

'Well, they've just put out the kotatsu table in the café for winter. The three of us could sit around it with a guest in the empty place,' said Tweed.

'And we'd call the guests forward one by one to join us at the table. Like at a doctor's surgery. We could even write out prescriptions for people!' I said.

We got so fired up by all this that we ended up deciding to hold the event. I would be the organiser, having come up with the idea in the first place. I knew it would be friends and people from the café, but still . . . Me, in charge of the whole event, collecting the attendance fee, inviting people to come along? I'd never have been able to imagine it a year ago. Could I really do it? Would anyone even show up? Could I come up with books to suit the café's idiosyncratic customers?

I couldn't deny that I was nervous, but I was excited, too. A three-on-one book recommendation jam around a kotatsu – I'd never heard of anything like it! The thrill I felt just imagining it was enough to overcome my nerves.

We started advertising the event in Café Hesomagari and on the café's blog, and I was relieved when several café regulars and friends from the co-working space expressed a desire to take part. The thought of nobody turning up at all was a stressful one, so I was very grateful to the people who were kind enough to say they'd be there.

The night before the event, I picked up my phone to find a missed call from my dad. My stomach lurched. We hardly ever contacted each other, and when we did it was usually via text. I hastily returned his call.

'Oh, Nanako? Thanks for calling back,' he said. There was a pause, and then he went on. 'Ah . . . Not long ago, ah . . . your grandpa passed away.'

'Oh. Oh . . .'

I knew Grandpa hadn't been well. When I'd visited him a week or so earlier, it was as though he'd been asleep the whole time, and I couldn't talk to him. I'd heard that sometimes people can hear you even if they can't respond, so before I left, I said,

'Grandpa, let's go out for a drink again sometime!' as loudly as I could. That was the last thing I'd said to him.

'The wake's tomorrow. Can you come home?'

'Tomorrow . . .? Tomorrow I've, um, I've got . . . something on . . . Um . . . I'm not sure . . .'

In the end, afraid of how it would sound, I couldn't mention something as frivolous as a book jam: not in the same conversation as my grandfather's wake. It was bad enough saying that I had 'something on'. Was I being unreasonable? It wasn't even as if my family lived far away – I could get there in an hour on the train.

I wasn't sure how my father had taken my reply: whether he'd given up on me, or whether he was just speechless. 'All right . . . well, it's up to you,' he said finally, and hung up.

I couldn't get my thoughts straight. I messaged Tweed and Sonton, whom I was supposed to be running the book jam event with.

'Hi guys. I actually just found out that my grandfather passed away today, and the wake is tomorrow. I don't know what to do! Should we postpone the book jam? People have already said they'll come . . .'

They were both extremely kind in their replies. Sonton's said: 'It's totally okay either way. I'm sure the customers will understand if we have to postpone, and they'll be happy to come again another time. Don't force yourself to do it if you don't feel like it, your feelings are the main thing here.'

'Yes. If we do decide to cancel or postpone, we can just get in touch with the people who said they'd take part. It's not a big deal,' went the message from Tweed.

I almost felt like crying at their thoughtfulness.

I got into bed for a bit, but I couldn't sleep. Instead, still in my comfy clothes, I draped a coat over my shoulders and went outside.

I liked walking from my place towards the Minato Mirai development on the waterfront. It reminded me of some apocalyptic landscape out of a film I'd seen a long time ago. Here and there, vacant lots gaped wide, overgrown with weeds, and the raised motorways swooped down low and criss-crossed over one another. Between the empty lots stood the occasional lonely train station or high-rise, giving the place a strange, futuristic feel. I walked along aimlessly, the only human in this silent space.

My beloved grandpa. I had been born to serious parents and brought up in a serious household, and at home he'd been my only ally, the only other person who didn't take everything seriously. He liked a drink, and during my uni days I often ran into him coming home on the last train. The rest of the family wondered, perplexed, just why the two of us came back so late nearly every night, what exactly it was we liked so much about hanging around in the city all the time. Once I'd grown up, my grandpa and I never went anywhere together. But when we bumped into each other coming back on the train, we would walk the short distance from the station to the house side by side. There was something special and calming about that time we spent tipsily wending our way home like co-conspirators.

Grandpa had been a regular at the Kamiya Bar in Asakusa, a long-standing establishment where they knew him by name. He took great pride in this. When I was a child, he told me – hundreds of times, it must have been – about a particular hope he had for us, and his worry that it would never happen.

'Nana-chan – I'd like to go drinking at Kamiya Bar with you and your boyfriend when you're older. But I bet when you grow up, you won't want to go out on the town with an old geezer like me!'

And every time, hundreds of times, I replied, 'Of course I will! You can take me there when I turn twenty and I've got a boyfriend for you to meet.'

It was the sort of thing that seemed easy enough to do any time, which meant ordinarily I might have ended up putting it off. In this case, though, unusually enough, it wasn't long before I actually did make arrangements to go out with Grandpa and my then-boyfriend. That particular relationship was long since over and we hadn't stayed in touch, but I was still truly glad he and I had been able to go out with my grandpa. If not, I would probably have regretted it for life. *I should have gone out with Grandpa more, though. Lots of times, just the two of us*, I thought.

I'd known Grandpa was going to pass away sooner or later, but that didn't stop a fresh sadness from welling up in my heart at the thought that he was no longer around.

Should I do the book jam? Or should I call it off? Could I really not go to the wake? Was I sure I wouldn't regret it afterwards if I didn't go?

After fretting and fretting, in the end I resolved to go through with the book jam. I decided to conveniently interpret this as a final message from my grandfather, my partner in crime. Maybe he was telling me to live my life freely? I knew Grandpa, and I knew without a doubt that he would have encouraged me to miss the wake in favour of staging my first real event. And if I could make *that* decision, then when I was faced with other, lesser dilemmas, it should be a piece of cake to choose whichever path led me to liberty.

After all, we'd formed a freedom alliance, we two comrades, even if my grandpa's dementia meant he might not have remembered it by the end. *Sorry, Grandpa*, I thought. *But I know you'll understand.*

*

The next morning, I opened the window to find the sky a breathtaking blue.

'Let's do the book jam as planned. Sorry for all the fuss,' I announced to Sonton and Tweed on Messenger. When I hit 'Send', my lingering misgivings melted away and I felt better.

My doubts resolved themselves like dominoes gently toppling one after another. *I'm glad I made this decision . . . It was the right choice . . . Or I'll try to see it that way, at least . . . Let's make this event one to remember.*

I hadn't imagined I would be going into the book jam on the back of having resolved to live freely, whatever that might mean. But there I was – about to face the first big event I'd ever organised in my life.

*

The little café was bustling. There were some familiar faces, but also plenty of people I was meeting for the first time today. Each one of them had taken the trouble to turn up. Each had been kind enough to show interest in our event, and to decide they might like to come along and get some book recommendations.

The customers were milling around as usual, sitting around the low kotatsu table drinking beer, or chatting away with each other. As the organiser, it was up to me to get proceedings underway.

'Hi, everyone, thank you all so much for joining us!' I said, in a loud voice that carried above the chatter. 'We're going to get started now! There are lots of people here today, so the plan is to give each person ten minutes of book chat. Now, if you could all line up in order . . . Okay – once the person in front of you has finished, we'll call you forwards to come and sit at the kotatsu!' And just like that, we were off.

Recommending books at Café Hesomagari wasn't like recommending books on PerfectStrangers. A lot of people I'd met through PerfectStrangers said they didn't read much. By contrast, most of the regulars at the café already had a keen interest in books and manga: they kept up with their favourite genres, and often had quite particular preferences. And we weren't just small-talking about books here, either: we were diving deep into the subject from the start. The way I'd gone about introducing books to my PerfectStrangers matches couldn't compare with the intensity and pace of what we were doing here.

Client number one was Yuka, a nineteen-year-old uni student.

'Do you have any ideas what kind of thing you'd like to read about?' I asked.

'Um . . . I'd like to know what love is,' Yuka replied.

This certainly caught the three of us off balance.

'Okay. Well . . . what kind of books do you normally read?' I said.

'Hmm . . . I guess I quite like Yukio Mishima. But in class recently, we were discussing *Wanderings in the Realm of the Seventh Sense* by Midori Osaki, and we got on to the question of what love is. The lecturer said the characters in the story were in love with love,' said Yuka.

'By any chance . . . does this relate to your own situation, in some way?' I ventured.

'Yes. There's this guy I really, really like.'

Having barely recovered ourselves, the three of us were caught off guard once more.

'Let's say he's called A,' Yuka explained. 'He liked this other girl, B. She already had a boyfriend, though, so I thought, okay, maybe I have a chance with A. But then B broke up with her boyfriend and started going out with A after all. So now I'm in the position of being a supportive friend to A and B in their relationship. Or rather I *was* – until B dumped A and got back together with her ex-boyfriend. And now A, who I still have feelings for, is bereft.'

I decided to get the ball rolling.

'I'd like to recommend Yuki Kurita's book *Terumi the Dressmaker*,' I said. 'I think this is an absolutely fantastic novel about unrequited love. A girl falls in love with a singer who's dressed up as a woman, but it can never be. The story is all about not making the person you love into an object, but living in a way that's worthy of them instead, and finding your own independence that way. It's about how seeing the person you love living beautifully can be a support to you in your own life.'

'Okay, I'm sold!' Yuka said.

Yes! One point to me! Not that we were keeping score, of course.

'Well, I'd like to introduce some books that give insight into the male mind,' said Sonton. 'How about Tomihiko Morimi's

The Night is Short, Walk on Girl; Ryu Murakami's *69*, and Keigo Higashino's *We Were Idiots Back Then*? Read these, and I think you'll see how men also get themselves twisted up in knots because they can't understand women.'

I followed up Sonton's rapid-fire recommendations with another title I'd thought of.

'Going back to unrequited love, Kanako Nishi's *White Mark* is also a good shout. This woman falls in love with someone she can't have, she's absolutely captivated, and then the instant her heart is broken, she just becomes completely blank. I think it's so real in the way it depicts what it's like to want a relationship that can never happen.'

Now it was Tweed's turn to join the fray.

'What you were saying earlier, Yuka – it made me think you might enjoy Plato's *Symposium*. It really gets into the nitty-gritty of passionate, romantic love, as well as love in a more altruistic, all-encompassing sense. The term "platonic love" comes from Plato.'

'Okay, so romantic desire versus *love* love,' Yuka said, nodding. 'Hmm. So what exactly do we mean by love in that wider sense, then . . .?'

We enjoyed giving some more serious thought to the topic, and then the first ten minutes were up.

The next person to sit down at the kotatsu was Tomoko, also a regular at Hesomagari. Everyone there loved her – she was almost like the café's mascot. 'Seeing as I have this opportunity,' she said, 'I want you to tell me whatever you think I should read, based on your first impressions of me.'

'That's a great idea! I wish someone would do the same for me!' I said, and Tweed and Sonton expressed similar sentiments. An entertaining challenge like this was just right for the book jam, and it really helped liven up the mood.

'My first impression says – Yoko Ogawa!' Tweed declared with great confidence.

'I can totally see that!' said Sonton.

I went next. 'I think an author like Yuriko Takeda. Or Françoise Sagan, maybe. If it's Yuriko Takeda, then start with *Fuji Diary*. And if it's Sagan, start with *Bonjour Tristesse*. It portrays that kind of particular coolness and cruelty that go along with adolescence, and I think it's got this atmosphere you just don't get in Japanese literature.'

'If you sit in a café reading Sagan, looking all cool and cruel, you'll definitely get some attention,' Sonton added, poking fun.

At some point we got diverted, and the question became, 'What should I read to make myself alluring?' Tomoko seemed to be enjoying herself, though.

'How about some manga? There's Fumiko Tanikawa,' I said. 'She's done lots of short stories, all aimed at adults. She draws these lovely romances, but they're not corny. My personal recommendation would be *Assertive* – it was also the book that got me interested in tanka poetry. And if you sat in a café reading it . . . yep, I'm pretty sure you'd look very beguiling.'

'Okay, well, I'll give all those a try, and see if I can increase my allure!' Tomoko giggled.

It was fun recommending books like this, just bantering away, going with the flow. It was partly the lively atmosphere and the fact I was among friends that made it so enjoyable. But I also liked it because, with three of us pitching titles, the discussion cracked along at a good pace. If I had to stop to think, the others picked up the slack. And, of course, we had triple the knowledge at our disposal.

Our next client was another young girl, Minori, who had been invited along by a friend. I immediately got the impression that she was quite a reader.

'I haven't really read books based on other people's recommendations before,' she said. 'I like Osamu Dazai, Ko Machida, Kenta Nishimura . . . I can get completely absorbed in their writing. But recently I haven't found any authors I've been able to get into in the same way.'

'I see. Well, what about Otaro Maijo?' said Tweed, kicking things off.

'I've read him already. I do like him, though.'

I promptly came to Tweed's aid, and for the next little while Minori and I were engaged in a rapid-fire ping-pong match.

'How about foreign literature?' I said. 'There's this author called Jack Ketchum, he wrote *The Girl Next Door*...'

'I've already read that one, sorry.'

'Hmm . . . What about Charles Bukowski?'

'I've tried him before, but I think I just wasn't that keen on the translation.'

'How about women writers? Do you know Izumi Suzuki?'

'Oh, yes, I like her.'

'Okay, okay, well what about manga? Arusen Shimure*, that's someone recent.'

'I'm already a fan!' said Minori.

'Oh, really? Okay. Hmm . . . How about *The Failed Lovers' Suicide at the Falls of Akame*, by Chokitsu Kurumatani?' I said.

'I liked it.'

'Right, right, okay . . . Just give me a minute, I need to have a think.' I'd hurled everything I had at Minori, but she'd sunk me. My teammates rallied round.

'Do you know Tomoko Yoshida?' asked Tweed.

'No, I haven't heard of her,' said Minori.

'You might like her. She recently released an anthology through a small press based in Aichi.'

'That's right,' said Sonton. 'And Ko Machida wrote a piece at the end of the book, a commentary, I guess, with some musings about the stories in the collection.'

'I see,' said Minori. 'Um . . . I wonder if, rather than recommending things I might like, it might be better to try something totally different? Japanese sci-fi, for example – that's

---

* Translator's note: In 2019, this manga artist changed his pen name to Wabisen Nanano.

something I know nothing about. Anything with quite a poetic style, I think I might enjoy.'

'Well, there's an author called Mado Nozaki who started out in the light-novel genre. His book *2* is good – it's a totally madcap story that attempts to define what makes the perfect film,' said Sonton.

The discussion had swung round in a different direction now, so I dusted myself off and dived back in.

'It might not be sci-fi, exactly, but when you said "poetic", it made me think of Kazuo Ishiguro,' I said.

'I've heard of him, but I've never read anything by him,' said Minori.

'Okay, perfect! Then I'd definitely recommend *Never Let Me Go*. On the surface, it's about the lives of these children at boarding school. But it's filled with this lurking sense of unease. It's like a mystery, you definitely don't want to read any spoilers beforehand. And by the end it really makes you think. Or really leaves a deep impression, I guess you could say.'

I'd got there too, in the end. I'd finally managed to come up with something Minori hadn't heard of.

Tweed took up the baton. 'How about Shinichi Hoshi or Tadashi Hirose? Shinichi Hoshi's "short-short stories" are easy to read, and Tadashi Hirose might be good if you'd like a longer novel. If you're thinking of getting into science fiction, those would be my recommendations.'

Then it was Sonton's turn. 'There are also the *Nova* short-story anthologies compiled by Nozomi Omori – there are about ten books. They feature loads of great authors – you might be able to find some more writers you like in there.'

'Oh, that sounds like a good lead,' said Minori. 'I'll definitely give them a try. Thank you!'

It had been a hellish ten minutes, but somehow we had made it out the other side.

My relief was short-lived, however, because we had more or less the same experience with the rest of the guests. It was as though we were playing on the highest difficulty setting, and I ended up quite out of breath. The requests were all things like, 'I want to read something interesting about linguistics,' and 'I've just finished reading Bolaño's 2666 and I want to know what to pick up next.' We even had a mentor of Sonton's, seemingly some sort of literary researcher who read around five hundred books a year, who'd come along to poke fun at him. My experiences on PerfectStrangers just couldn't compare: here, our guests kept returning fire with, 'I know that one,' or 'I've already read it,' or 'That's not quite what I'm looking for.' As soon as one of us had to pause for thought, the next would valiantly follow up with another book they'd thought of. We did this again and again and again, and with the three of us combined, we just about managed to stay on top of it all.

It was hard going, and it was a struggle – but not *really*, not in a bad way. Maybe it was because Café Hesomagari was such a friendly space, but we found ourselves joking about silly nonsense with the guests, and going off on complete tangents. Other customers joined in the conversation, and some kind soul took pity on us and brought the three of us a drink – the event was an absolute blast from beginning to end.

More animated than usual and fuelled by adrenaline, the three of us had talked non-stop for more than three hours and recommended books to a total of fifteen customers. We had managed to get round all of our guests, and when I announced the end of the event and thanked everyone for coming, the little venue filled with applause.

I was exhausted, burnt out. I felt like I would turn into white ash, just like *Tomorrow's Joe* after the fight of his life. I looked over at my colleagues and saw they were both similarly spent, their gazes vacant, their faces betraying total fatigue.

We stood at the door and waved off those who'd stayed until the very end.

I caught Minori's eye as she left, and couldn't help flagging her down. I'd managed to recommend her one thing she hadn't read, at least, but it bothered me a bit that we hadn't been more helpful.

'Minori, um . . . Sorry we didn't manage to think of many books for you.'

'That's okay, I had such a good time anyway. Yeah – it was a lot of fun!' she said.

'Oh, that's great! I didn't think we'd been much use to you . . .'

'I really love books, but usually no one around me gets it,' said Minori. 'So hearing all these different titles, being able to talk properly about books for the first time – it made me very happy.'

Her reply took me by surprise, and really stuck in my mind.

I think that perhaps up until then, I'd had a slightly condescending attitude when it came to introducing people to new books.

After all, it required a good grasp of the literary landscape, naturally, as well as the ability to analyse the other person, to read them, and I'd been using all the skills I had at my disposal to make my suggestions. I didn't believe simple enthusiasm could make up for a lack of knowledge, I thought that was too naive, and when I used PerfectStrangers, I found myself frustrated by my own inability and lack of expertise on more than a few occasions.

But even if you had knowledge, even if you had analytical ability, there was still something missing.

If I viewed recommending books to people through a lens of superiority, if I saw it as me bestowing knowledge on people who knew less than me, then when I met someone whose knowledge outstripped mine, I would cease to have any value. Surely this wasn't what I'd had in mind.

While recommending books on PerfectStrangers, I'd been curious to see exactly how the other pros went about it, and I'd perused book reviews in magazines to find out. I read reviews by well-known booksellers and was disappointed. They only wrote about whether or not something was a bestseller, how many thousands of copies it had sold, which awards it had won. When it came to what was actually *in* the book, the explanation was perfunctory: only what you'd find on the book's blurb, or its Amazon page. There was no hint of the reviewer's own opinion, no suggestion as to what exactly made the book worth reading. And yet these booksellers *must* have plenty of expertise. Maybe they tried to avoid making themselves the focus of the review. Still – where among those reviews had they actually tried to communicate to anyone why they should pick up a book?

These book reviews are lifeless, I'd thought.

And there was one other thing that had always niggled away at me. It was the thought that I'd matched with so many people on PerfectStrangers and recommended them books, but there must be some who hadn't read theirs. I'd met dozens of people by now, and it seemed unlikely that they'd all have taken the trouble to buy and read whatever I'd picked. Based on the general feeling I got, I reckoned maybe half my matches had read their books. So did that mean half of my recommendations had been completely pointless?

I still wanted each and every recommendation, each and every book, to be of some use to those people – even if they never actually read it.

This led me to devise a strategy that went something like this: *You're wonderful and this book is wonderful, therefore I'm recommending this wonderful book to wonderful you.*

Say you happen to be passing by a designer shop somewhere in the city, and displayed in pride of place in the window is this beautiful, dazzling dress. It catches your eye and you admire it, and then your friend or your partner who's with you says, 'I think it'd really suit you!'

Wouldn't that make you happy? Maybe you'd feel bashful; 'I've got nowhere to go in such an expensive dress,' you might say, or 'I don't have the waist for it.' But you'd feel a little glow of happiness, because you'd know what your companion is really telling you is that they think you're as wonderful as the dress.

They're saying, *You're the sort of lovely person who'd suit that lovely dress.* So just by existing there behind the glass, the dress is providing you with value, even if you never actually wear it. I thought I could use books to achieve the same thing.

And so I'd begun to introduce books in a different way. First, I'd tell my match about all the good qualities I saw in them. Then I'd draw a connection between those things and the book I had chosen. And then I'd explain how the book could help them.

'From what you've said, I feel like you're someone who tries to make other people happy through your work. You really think about what's best for your colleagues and customers, and you power through life, always giving your absolute best. So, here's the book I want to suggest to you. When you're worrying about your work, and when things seem difficult, I think this book will speak to you and be a support to you.'

With this approach, I thought whoever was receiving the recommendation could consider their as-yet-unread book as a sort of a talisman, quietly waiting for its moment. It was okay if they didn't buy the book – but if they did, and if they even just laid eyes upon it now and again, that was enough.

If, in some corner of their mind, they retained the thought that when things got tough, they could read this book and it would help bring them back to being the wonderful person they were – if they could do that, it would be like I was there beside them, talking to them again, and the value of what I had done would finally manifest itself.

Having said all that, we'd really just been clowning around at Café Hesomagari. I felt ashamed at how little I'd actually been able to achieve, despite all my high ideas.

I found myself coming to the natural conclusion that, for now, I was going to stop recommending books to strangers. I was tired after the book jam, of course, having chattered on and on excitedly until the words dried up. But more than that, I was left with an abounding sense that I had now taken this experiment as far as I needed. It felt liberating, in a way: as though I were out for a run and had decided that since I'd done 5K, it was time to call it a day. And I'd made some progress on my warrior's quest, hadn't I?

After all, until I'd started all of this, recommending books had been just that: recommending books. Nothing more, and nothing less.

And so I took out my phone and deleted the shortcut to PerfectStrangers from my home screen.

EPILOGUE

ENDINGS AND BEGINNINGS

I'd been habitually checking the job sites, and one day a particular ad caught my eye. It was for a role in the large book department of a big, newly opened showroom store that also sold things like homeware and appliances. They were looking for staff who could bring books and customers together, people with diverse experience. It was fine if you'd never worked in a bookshop before, they said; they welcomed those with unusual CVs. I clicked to see more, and found that even in the 'Further details' section they were insisting, 'Use the interview to tell us all about your experiences and what makes you different.'

Well, all right then. I decided to go all in. In the 'Tell us about yourself' section of the application form I wrote, 'I used a dating site to meet all sorts of different people in real life, talked to each person for half an hour, and then introduced them to the book I thought would suit them perfectly. In the last year, I've met and recommended books to more than seventy people.' Form complete, I hit 'Submit'. I got a sense that the company culture might be quite liberal, so I thought my application stood a chance. Although maybe it wasn't as easy as that, and they'd just reject it.

My application, however, passed swiftly through the screening stage, and I was invited for an interview.

The first interview was a group one: three interviewees and seven people from the company. I sat in between the other two hopeful applicants. The person on my left was a former local councillor, and the person on my right had been editor-in-chief at a publishing house, and was now managing a famous musician. And then there was me, sandwiched between these two high fliers. Was that the calibre of people this job was attracting? Maybe I'd miscalculated. I lost all confidence in my utterly mediocre CV.

It was my turn to speak. I talked briefly about why I'd applied for the job, and about my previous work experience. Finally, one of the interviewers sprung a question on me.

'So, Nanako, you've been working for Village Vanguard for quite a while, ever since graduating university – more than ten years. Now that you're thinking of leaving and potentially coming to work with us, what sort of frame of mind are you in?'

What sort of frame of mind was I in . . . ? I took an honest look at my feelings.

'Village Vanguard . . .' I began, my voice shaking. 'Village Vanguard was the place that taught me the joy of work, and how fun it was to sell things, and how to collaborate with colleagues and support each other . . . I'd never *been* anything before, but Village Vanguard taught me everything. It's not quite the right place for me anymore, so I've decided to leave, but – but right now, I just feel so grateful.'

As I finished, the tears welled up. I'd thought through my decision over and over again and my mind was made up; I was sure in my heart that it was the right thing to do. But every time I followed this train of thought, I started crying. Even now, in the middle of an interview.

Surely they weren't going to hire someone this emotionally unstable? Especially not someone who'd made the dubious decision to mention their dating-site escapades on their application form. In the end, I couldn't bring myself to talk about PerfectStrangers at all.

And yet, contrary to my expectations, I soon received word that I'd passed the first round of interviews. And the second round of interviews, they said, was the final one.

On the day of the final interview I found myself in the same small conference room as before. This time, the only other people there were a man and woman from the company who had both been there in the previous round. This made me feel better, and I relaxed a little.

The two of them were apparently team leaders for the new store. No sooner had they introduced themselves than the man said, through stifled laughter, 'All right, Nanako, to tell you the truth – I just couldn't wait to hear more about you today!'

'Um, really?' I said. 'Do you mean, about the dating site?'

'The dating site! She just goes ahead and says it like it's normal!' He chuckled. 'Honestly, we all looked at your application, and everyone was talking about it. We've got a right one here, we thought!'

'Most people wouldn't do something like that,' said the woman. 'I think it's amazing. It just goes to show what an incredible passion you have for books, Nanako.'

'Oh . . . do you think so?'

They were acting as though I'd done something commendable, which couldn't be a bad thing. But all I could think about was me playing Werewolf at the co-working space, or practising the art of picking up men. Those didn't exactly seem like the sort of noble achievements you'd be lauded for in an interview. And anyway – had all those things I'd done really come from my passion for books? I didn't think that was quite true.

'We heard all about your work at Village Vanguard in the first interview – that helped with our decision too, of course. But really, how could we not hire someone with such an interesting story? We've got to have at least one eccentric on the team. We need a bit of that maverick energy around here!' The man chuckled again.

The two of them were both grinning. Wait – so that meant . . . ?

'Now, if we could talk to you about the genres you'll be in charge of . . .' continued the woman.

It was an abrupt notification of hire, to say the least.

I'd mentioned PerfectStrangers in the job application in the hope it would work in my favour, of course, but still . . . Who else could say they'd been hired because they'd mentioned their dating site on their CV? Incredible. Maybe the world was a friendlier place than I'd realised.

I'd thought my job search was going to drag on forever – but suddenly it was over, just like that.

*

The sky was overcast, threatening rain any minute.

It had been a while since I'd got off at this station – although it was only a year, so of course it hadn't really changed much.

I met my husband in a Renoir café in Nishinippori, not far from where we used to live. I handed him the divorce papers I'd prepared. The café was empty, but he took a quick glance at my signature and then quickly stowed the papers in his bag, as though he didn't want anyone else to see.

'I'll fill in the rest today and take it to the ward office tomorrow. It looks like they're open at weekends,' he said.

'That's great. Thanks.'

And then it was a matter of squaring our accounts. We had saved up some money together. When we separated, my husband had moved into a shared house; he had his own room, but the kitchen and everything were communal. I'd taken the large furniture and appliances and was getting to keep most of them, so we took that into account when working out how to split our savings.

We calculated it so that I would pay roughly half the original price of any big purchases. The fridge had cost 110,000 yen; the TV, 80,000 yen; the sofa we'd bought at Karimoku, 50,000 yen . . . The portion I owed was deducted from our savings, and then we split the remaining balance. After we'd both double-checked the figure, we went to the Sumitomo Mitsui cashpoint around the corner. I withdrew the money and handed my husband his share, and then it was all over.

We began a tentative conversation, neither of us really taking the lead. *Whereabouts are you living now? How's the new job? I saw so-and-so recently. Oh really, is he doing well?* I wasn't sure if we were really interested in talking about these things, or if we were just going through the motions. Once we'd more or less run out of small talk, my husband said, 'I know it might not be possible right now, but at some point, once things have settled down, it might be nice to have dinner now and again.'

'Yes, it would,' I said.

When I came out with the old clichéd 'Well, thank you for everything,' it felt like a sign the conversation was drawing to a close.

'Well, thank you, too,' he said.

'I'm sorry about everything.'

'No, I'm sorry as well.'

'We had lots of good times, though.'

'Yeah, it was always a lot of fun.'

It felt like a truthful exchange, but it also felt as though we were following a script so we could wrap things up amicably. 'Thank you,' 'Thank you,' the two of us repeated, until the words sounded strange and seemed to lose all meaning. I couldn't help feeling we were just filling in time so we wouldn't end up saying anything else, so we wouldn't let too much emotion come into it – trying not to ruin the mood at the very end, at least.

We parted in front of the cashpoint – not much of a place for a goodbye, either.

'Well, see you. Take care,' I said, waving as I hurried off.

I made as if to head for the station, but then I went by myself to see the place where the two of us had lived. From across the busy road, I peered up at our old sixth-floor flat. It looked like someone new had moved in. Behind the closed windows hung unfamiliar blue curtains.

How had it come to this? When we'd had such good times together? The tears sprang to my eyes. But once I'd cried it out and the tears had dried up for the time being, I thought, *All right. Well, it's over now.*

*

'Finally got divorced!' I sent to Endo on LINE.

This was several days later. The message soon showed as read.

'Nice!' was Endo's reply, casual as ever. I'd never seen him send a message of more than one line. Or so I was thinking when he tagged on another: 'Let's get dinner to celebrate!'

And so he booked us a private booth in an upmarket izakaya, and we met for drinks.

We raised our glasses to each other across the table.

'Wahey! Well done,' Endo said. He cheerfully clinked his glass against mine, either with his natural good humour, or because he was being nice and trying to liven up the mood.

'Well, how's it feel?' he asked.

'Mmm . . . It feels sad, definitely. But I think it's also kind of a relief,' I said.

'Makes sense, I guess. But you'll be fine, Nanako! I mean, it's not like that's your love life over.'

'I suppose not . . .'

'Got anyone new in mind?' asked Endo. 'I hear divorcees are much sought after, you know.'

'Hey, Endo,' I said.

'Yeah?'

'Do you ever feel like you want to sleep with me? I want to know what you think.'

Endo spat out his drink – *ptooey* – like a cartoon character. 'Wait, what is this – are we having a fun jokey talk right now? Or a scary talk?' he said.

'It's not really either,' I said. 'I just wondered if you ever thought about it at all.'

'Okay, well, I'll say this – if you wanted to sleep with me, then I would! But I don't feel like that's the vibe we have going. So maybe things are fine the way they are, you know?'

'Okay . . . sorry if I sound like a teenager here, but that means you don't really have feelings for me, right?' I said.

'Wait, hang on. Are you upset?'

'No, not at all. I just want to be clear.'

'Do I have feelings for you . . .?' Endo pondered. 'Well, I do like you a lot. What do you mean exactly, feelings? Are you saying that's what you want?'

'No, that's not really it . . . I guess I just wondered if things are fine with us the way they are. I'm not sure how I'd feel about a relationship and stuff either. I just know it's fun hanging out with you like this sometimes. You're the friend I rely on most right now.'

'Score!'

'But I don't think I'm really into the idea of going out on a date every week, or being cutesy and getting each other presents because it's a year since we first met, or anything like that.'

'No, me neither. So we're good! Or are you bringing this up because *you* want to have sex, by any chance? Fine by me – let's head to a hotel!' he joked, grinning and wiggling his eyebrows.

'Nope, I don't think so.'

'Aww, boo.'

'I mean, if you were to ask me whether I could do it with you or not, I definitely could.'

'Nice!'

'The problem is...'

'Uh-huh? What?'

'I guess I just don't have that much appetite for sex at the moment...' I said.

Endo had been leaning forwards across the table at this point, but now he gave a great, exaggerated sigh and slumped back in his chair.

'Come on, don't say that!' he said.

'What? Why not?'

'I mean, there's nothing more disheartening than when a girl drinking with you says she's got no appetite for sex. Even if you're never going to sleep with a guy, he can survive on the hope that it might be possible! It doesn't have to be for me, but if you say things like, "Yeah, lately I'm just super turned on!", you'll make a guy really happy.'

I had never heard this singular theory before. But I could tell it was stupid.

'As long as I can imagine that someday your feelings might change and then it might happen, that's enough for me. I'll buy you a meal with an open heart!' said Endo.

'Oh yeah, thanks for treating me,' I said. 'Seriously, though, is all that stuff really true? I thought guys didn't like getting their hopes up for nothing.'

'Of course it's true. The best woman is the one who's always just out of your reach!'

'Oh right, okay. Not sure about that. I'll do my best to give you hope, though,' I said flippantly.

'Amazing!' said Endo, missing my tone and getting further carried away. 'Well, if you end up with so much sex drive that literally anyone will do, let me know! Oh yeah, and then we can visit one of those sex clubs! I've always wanted to go at least once.'

It looked like his imagination was already running wild.

Thinking back on it, we could have slept with each other on the very first night we met, but neither of us had come on strong or attempted to take things in that direction. So maybe the pair of us had good communication skills, but a low capacity for romance. There were no sexual feelings, but we were able to talk openly and the relationship was a comfortable one.

'Well, look, I know I'm saying all this stuff – but I'm sure you'll find someone great, Nanako. And I really want you to be happy!' Endo said. He spoke as though he was still messing about, but I knew he meant it, and I was touched.

And anyway, maybe I should be grateful that I had some insurance if the time ever came when I wanted to have sex so badly that anyone would do. Still, I got the feeling that it would probably never happen – that things would always be like this between us.

'I'm glad you seem happy, anyway,' he said.

'What do you mean? About the divorce?'

'Well, that, and everything. When I met you, your job seemed to be getting you down, too. But you're moving ahead now.'

'Yeah, thanks to your help.'

'What're you on about? I didn't do anything!' Endo laughed it off, and then flagged down a member of staff and ordered another round of beer.

Evenings like this, friendship like this, were what sustained me.

*

It was only February, but it was unseasonably mild, like a spring day.

Today, I was saying goodbye to this city: to Yokohama. I suppose I could have commuted to my new job in Tokyo from there, but I had been renting my flat through work, so when I left I would have had to temporarily vacate the place anyway. Going through the necessary admin to stay on there was a faff, so I'd decided to move somewhere closer to my new workplace instead.

My most pressing issue just now was that the movers would be here in three hours, and I was nowhere near finished packing. I frantically set to stuffing things in boxes, but there was absolutely no chance I would be ready in time.

Then I got a message from Tetsu, who lived nearby.

'I saw a book on your shelf yesterday I'd like to read, have you already packed up your stuff? If you have it's totally fine, don't worry about it. I just thought maybe I could borrow it – I could pick it up when I return your other books. I can give it back to you later at your new job.'

Why had I left things so late? I'd told myself yesterday I was going to really crack on with the packing, but then a bunch of people from the co-working space had come round, and we'd ended up having a Mario Kart tournament on the Super Famicom.

Ever since I'd decided to move away, my friends from the co-working space had been coming over day after day to hang out. Tetsu was one of them. We all played video games, and did hotpot in the dark, with people bringing over random secret ingredients to add to the pot. The fact that I would soon be leaving made the time feel like a summer holiday, one that I knew would eventually come to an end. My grown-up friends always seemed to take midnight as their cue to leave my flat, the way primary-school kids know it's home time when they hear the chimes at the end of the day. When it got to twelve, someone or other would say, 'Well, I guess we should head off . . .?' and they'd all file out together.

Friends were coming over on a daily basis now, making themselves at home in my flat, casually helping themselves out of my fridge, reorganising my bookshelves. There was something so enlivening about it all. Every day was fun, and it was like I actually had real fulfilment in my home life. When my friends left and my flat fell silent, the loneliness surged in around me – but I liked to savour that solitude, too.

Anyway, I'm ashamed to say that I now decided to take advantage of Tetsu.

'If you come over right now I'll give you the book!' I sent.

Tetsu duly came round and was enlisted in helping me pack. He ended up staying until the movers arrived, and got stuck helping me take out the rubbish and do the hoovering. The movers actually thought he was the tenant, and they kept asking him which things they were meant to be taking to the new place and which were going out.

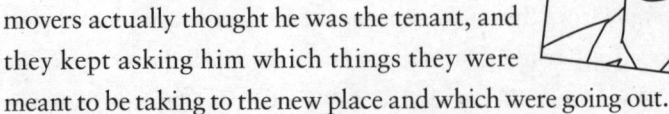

By the time Tetsu was finally released, the sun was starting to set and the sky had turned orange.

'Oh, that's weird,' he said. 'Look at the time. And I thought I only came over to borrow a book . . .'

I realised that having been relocated with work time and time again meant that up until now I'd never made friends in my local area. And when I moved, of course, I wouldn't know anyone in the new place either.

How did I end up getting to know so many people in Yokohama? I wondered, and then I remembered it was because I'd met Esaki on PerfectStrangers, and he'd invited me along to the co-working space, where I'd made friends with everyone.

Even without PerfectStrangers, perhaps I could have made friends locally if I had wanted to. It was just that it had never even occurred to me before. So which version of me was the real one? After all, I was naturally shy around new people, wasn't I?

I'd built up so many connections in Yokohama now. Unlike all the other places I'd lived, it just didn't feel like this would be the last time I was here.

*

I parted with Tetsu at the crossroads, thanking him again and again and feeling like I should get down and prostrate myself on the ground in gratitude.

'Thanks for the book. I'll come and visit you at your new job!' he said.

'I'm sure I'll be back to hang out with everyone soon. See you again!' I replied.

As the sky above darkened from orange to purple, I set out on foot for Yokohama Station.

By the time I had finished getting all my things into the new flat, it was completely dark outside. I unpacked the items I'd need straight away, plugged in the TV and shoved everything to one side so I had somewhere to sleep. Before I knew it, it was gone eleven.

I realised I was hungry, so I took my purse and ventured out into the unfamiliar night-time streets. I had to laugh at myself – I didn't have a clue where anything actually was.

I crossed a small bridge and wandered along aimlessly until I arrived at a main road, where I found a solitary family restaurant, a chain I'd never heard of before. Checking it was still open, I went inside. Despite the lateness of the hour, there were several couples and groups of students in there, chatting away merrily as they ate.

I placed my order and then sat and looked out into the night. Unfamiliar, empty buses in a different colour than I was used to slid past the window. I had arrived somewhere else now. I imagined myself catching these buses, in this new place, in my new life.

I always think being in a family restaurant late at night is like being in a spaceship. No matter how you're feeling inside, it just holds you there, gently, cocooned in the night.

A year ago, I'd been sitting in another restaurant like this, in despair and with nowhere to go. It had felt like my life held no joy. I'd clenched my trembling hands and leaned forwards to try and peer into the turbulent river, and then I'd tumbled in and been swept away, onwards and onwards, gripped by the powerful current; and when I came round, I found I had been washed up here, and I could no longer recall that place I'd left behind. People say women are ruthless because they cast off the past so quickly. I certainly was: I no longer shed sentimental tears at the thought of my marriage, and I was sure that, as extraordinary and precious as this past year had been, one day I would forget all about it too.

Maybe this sensation of hurtling along at full speed was the only proof to me that I was alive. But there was something sad about that. Perhaps that was why I had such a powerful urge to come into contact with other people's lives, even if only for a fleeting moment. To be allowed to exist within someone else for a little while.

'Here you go.'

The tantalising smell of freshly cooked food tickled my nose, and my wandering train of thought was cut off as my plate was placed down in front of me.

*

Just like that last time, today, too, marked the beginning of something new. Would I be swept off my feet once more, forever being carried off somewhere new? Well, then – let me be swept away, as far as I could possibly go. Let the current take me anywhere it liked.

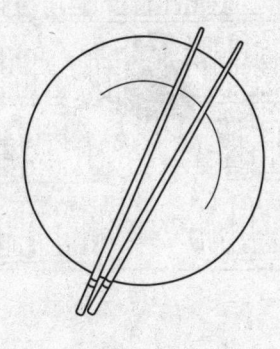

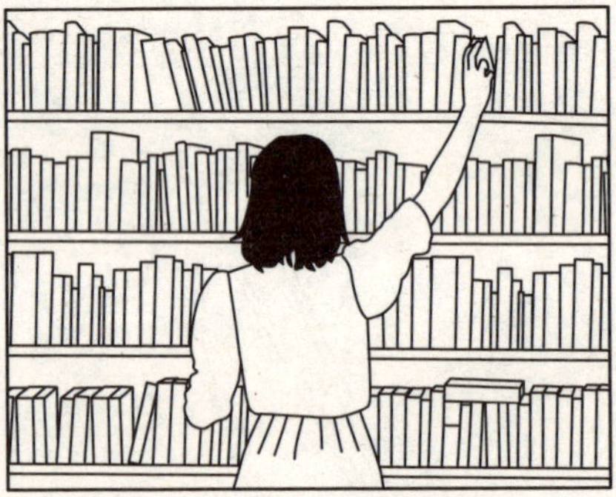

AFTERWORD

AUTUMN 2017, IN A BOOKSHOP

I worked at the large book-slash-homeware store for a while, but after a few years, I quit that job too and became the manager of a small bookshop in an old neighbourhood in east Tokyo.

Being in a little bookshop rather than a big one meant I could chat to the customers to my heart's content and just enjoy the slow passage of time. Recommending books to the customers was clearly a continuation of what I'd been doing on PerfectStrangers; the difference was that here, people were actually handing over their money to buy the books. And what delighted me most of all was that my relationships with the customers continued.

Customers came back to the shop and told me with excitement how they'd really enjoyed the books I'd suggested last time. I chatted to them each time they visited and gradually got a handle on what they liked. And then, even when they hadn't requested anything, I would find myself thinking, *I bet so-and-so would like that new book, maybe I'll order in a copy*, or *I wonder if so-and-so will be in again next week? Which book shall I recommend to her next? This one might be good . . .*

The customers and I started out as total strangers, but as we opened up to each other more and more, our connections deepened, and this felt more worthwhile to me than anything else. Increasingly I found that the customers were the ones recommending *me* books: 'Nanako, have you read this? I think you'd like it . . .'

It wasn't as though I'd always been dead set on working in a bookshop and nowhere else – it was just the way things had turned out. The result, though, was that I started to really enjoy recommending books as a job, more than I had done four years earlier.

I had for some time been writing about my experiences in a series of articles for the site WEBmagazine Ondo.

The series was announced on Twitter, and I watched the number of retweets grow and grow. I was in a state of turmoil, more shocked than delighted. After about two days, when the turmoil subsided, I started to feel properly happy about it.

To think that all these people I didn't know were reading my story, and retweeting it, and writing nice things on their timelines about how interested they were, and wondering what would happen next! To think that this thing I'd written had actually struck a chord with people! I couldn't believe it. I was elated. I just wanted to roll around on my futon, waving my arms and legs in the air.

So that was how things stood when I began writing up my experiences. I'd begun writing in a pretty laid-back way, thinking it might be nice if a few friends were interested in reading it, so I was taken aback by the unexpected success. I hadn't anticipated the level of response I got, and it certainly surprised me – but generally speaking, those were peaceful days.

It was a Sunday in autumn. More than half of the material that would later become this book must have been serialised online at that point.

I was in the shop sitting behind the till, when a customer came up to me: a lady about my age.

'I saw you on Twitter today, and I read your series about the dating site and came here because I wanted to meet you. I was wondering if you could pick out a book for me . . .' she said.

I see, I thought. *So this is what happens when word gets round on Twitter!*

'Oh, really? Well, thank you for visiting,' I said. 'What kind of book are you looking for?'

But the lady didn't reply. She just went quiet.

What was going on? Was she a little bit strange? Or was she just thinking? I looked at her, about to say something, when I saw that it was neither. It was that she was struggling to hold back tears while she tried to get her next words out.

I watched her quietly. After a little while, she managed to speak through her sobs.

'I recently, l-lost, my mum . . . S-So I wanted, something to read . . .' Only a few words, but it looked as though it had cost her a lot just to get them out.

Putting myself in her shoes, I knew at times like these it was reassuring to be with someone who didn't get upset by your tears and end up an emotional wreck themselves. This was something I'd learned first hand a while ago from Yukari, the life coach. So I did my best to remain composed as I led the lady over to the bookshelves.

'There are lots of books I'd love to introduce to you. Let's see . . . What kind of thing do you normally read? Do you read much?' I said.

'I don't read all that often. I might not manage anything very long or difficult . . .'

'All right. Well, then, I think it really depends on how you want the book to make you feel.'

First, I picked up *My Life Today*, by Miri Masuda, and showed her the cover.

'If you're hurting, and you want something to relieve you and take you away from your sadness for a little while, if you want to take a bit of time out, then I think this manga would be a good choice. It manages all of that, but without ignoring the tough things or forcing the humour. The author also talks about when her own father passed away, so I think there will be a lot in there that makes sense to you. It's the kind of thing that might help you feel positive, and more ready to accept your own emotional turmoil and fragility.'

Then from another shelf I picked out Nao-Cola Yamazaki's *Beautiful Distance*, and from the stock drawer I took out Kentaro Ueno's *Without Even Saying Goodbye*. I held both out.

AUTUMN 2017, IN A BOOKSHOP

'If you want to look that sadness you're feeling right in the eye, then maybe try this novel, *Beautiful Distance*. The main character is a husband who's caring for his wife when she's diagnosed with cancer quite young. It's not made into a big, overly sentimental drama or anything – it just takes a calm, clear-eyed view of ordinary life, of being with a partner, of the emotional changes you go through . . . It talks about everything from his wife's hospitalisation to her death and the funeral, so it might be quite close to home for you at the moment, and there are lots of bits that will make you cry. But I think it might help you process your feelings.

'And if you want to let all that sadness out, *really* let it out, then I'd definitely recommend *Without Even Saying Goodbye*. It's another manga – the art style is a little bit masculine, but if you don't mind that . . . The author depicts his day-to-day life following his wife's sudden death from an illness. He just draws and draws and draws it all, the unbearable sadness and the way his everyday life has been completely turned upside down. It really brings home just how hard it is to lose someone you love.'

The woman's tears had subsided a little, and she was listening closely to my explanations.

'Take some time to have a look at them all, if you like,' I said. 'I hope one of them might be right for you.'

Nodding, she took the books from me and began perusing them. I quietly returned to the till so she could be by herself.

After a short while, she brought over *Beautiful Distance* and *Without Even Saying Goodbye*. I thought her choice spoke of how she must have been feeling when she decided to come here today, and this put me on the verge of tears too. So she didn't want to forget about how she felt, or find a little comfort; she wanted to steadily face that sorrow, to delve down into it, and that was why she'd come here looking for a book.

It happened from time to time. Sometimes when I was recommending books, I would inadvertently get a glimpse of something deep in a person's heart – a strong emotion or significant event, a trauma caused by a difficult incident in the past, a complex or a feeling of inferiority they'd been holding onto all this time, or a sense of loss that was deeply affecting their life.

When this happened, I tried to act with as much sincerity and objectivity as I could. I did my best not to be shocked or to overreact, but to just gently accept whatever was in their heart.

Anyway, the most important thing was that I'd been able to come up with some books that the customer had liked – and, speaking more practically, that we'd actually had in stock.

When that particular visit occurred, *My Life Today* had only just come out and was selling well in the shop, so we always had it in stock. *Beautiful Distance*, however, had been published more than a year ago, and as slightly older books didn't sell so quickly, I'd only been keeping one copy in. I knew I'd sold a copy recently, but my memory had been hazy about whether its replacement had arrived yet. And I loved *Without Even Saying Goodbye*, so I'd made sure it was on the shelves when we first opened the shop, but it didn't sell all that well and it didn't seem to gel well with the other books around it, either. I thought I had put it back in the stock drawer – but I hadn't gone and returned it, had I? Unlike with PerfectStrangers, if we didn't have the actual books I was recommending right here and right now, then the whole thing was pointless.

So when I did find those two books, I secretly breathed a sigh of relief.

The lady thanked me as I rang up her purchases on the till. I felt suddenly curious, and without really knowing why, I asked, 'Have you come far today?'

'From Niigata,' she said. I felt giddy. *But that's hours away.*

If I could be of some use to a stranger in this way, then in the end, that was the happiest feeling there was. Though, of course, there was no guarantee I'd be able to meet everyone's expectations every time.

It's difficult, getting involved with another person just on the strength of your desire to help them, to be useful. If someone is struggling, you can't exactly say to them, 'I hope you feel okay soon!' or 'I'm sure better things are on the way!' even if you genuinely mean it. Especially not if they're a stranger.

But when I introduce books, I can exchange my sentiments with people I don't know without forcing my own feelings on them. If that lady hadn't been able to come and ostensibly ask me about books, she might never have confided in me about the thing that was weighing on her most heavily, and I might never have shed my own tears for her mother's death. I might never have witnessed her determination to fully confront her sadness, nor been able to give her any support.

That's why I like books. And why I like working in bookshops, where I can share those books with people.

However, never for a moment did I imagine that my own very personal, madcap journey would end up in a book itself.

And who knows? Maybe, just maybe, the day will come when one person picks up this book of mine and recommends it to someone else. It could be the start of an infinite loop . . . Well, sort of. The story would be circulating, anyway – and that's pretty incredible.

In fact, I can't think of anything more wonderful.

BOOKS RECOMMENDED IN THIS BOOK

Chapter 1

Sex in Japan, Takehiro Higuchi (Futaba Bunko)*
Telling You How I Feel: The Complete Exhibition, Ellie Omiya (Foil)*
Women's Words, Noriko Ibaragi (Dowa-ya Poetry Bunko)*
The Art of Funny, Shohei Kobayashi, Shuji Yamamoto and Keiya Mizuno (Shincho Bunko)*
The Road to Meets: The Age of the Neighbourhood Magazine, Hiroki Ko (Hon no Zasshi-sha)*

Chapter 2

What Am I? From Individual to Dividual, Keiichiro Hirano (Kodansha Gendai Shinsho)*
Wild Mountain, Hideyasu Moto (Ikki Comix)*
Poten Life, Shinya Kinoshita (Morning KC)*
Cities, Consumption and the Disney Dream: The Age of Shopping-Mallisation, Kenro Hayamizu (Kadokawa One Tema 21)*

*Books with an asterisk are not available in English at time of translation.

Chapter 3

Cosmic Profit: How to Make Money Without Doing Time, Raymond Mungo (Little, Brown and Company)
Make Your Work!, Yoshiaki Nishimura (Chikuma Bunko)*
Build Your Own Independent Nation, Kyohei Sakaguchi, translated by Corey Turpin and Kaz Egashira (Doyosha)
Living Freely on 1.5 Million Yen a Year, Hayato Ikeda (Seikaisha Shinsho)*
The Happy Youth of a Desperate Country: The Disconnect Between Japan's Malaise and Its Millenials, Noritoshi Furuichi, translated by Raj Mahtani (Japan Publishing Industry Foundation for Culture)
Into the Wild, Jon Krakauer (Pan Macmillan)
Illusions: The Adventures of a Reluctant Messiah, Richard Bach (Cornerstone)
The Children's Story, James Clavell (Blackstone Publishing)
Bare Naked Girls' Talk: Love, Sex and Beauty for the Around-Thirties, Artesia (BellSystem24; later partially reprinted in *Artesia's Girls' Night In*, Gentosha Bunko)*
Mojacko, Fujiko F Fujio (Shogakukan)*
What Did You Eat? Correspondence between Hiromi Ito and Nahomi Edamoto, Hiromi Ito and Nahomi Edamoto (Chuko Bunko)*

Chapter 4

On the Road, Jack Kerouac (Penguin Books)
The Grown-Ups' Short-Essay Course, Zoonie Yamada (Kawade Bunko)*
Beauty and the Beast: How to Be the Beast, Keiya Mizuno (Bunshun Bunko)*
Undiscardable People, George Akiyama (Gentosha Bunko)*

Chapter 5

Midnight Express, Kotaro Sawaki (Shincho Bunko)*

BOOKS RECOMMENDED IN THIS BOOK

Chapter 6

The Chronicle of the Woman Who Sings Bossa Nova Covers of Those J-pop Songs They Always Play in Cafés, Chokkaku Shibuya (Fusosha)*
I'm Only Here for the Deep-Fried Oysters, Sekishiro and Naoki Matayoshi (Gentosha Bunko)*

Chapter 7

Sightseeing, Rattawut Lapcharoensap (Atlantic Books)
Youth and Perversity, Makoto Aida (Chikuma Bunko)*
Terumi the Dressmaker, Yuki Kurita (Shueisha Bunko)*
White Mark, Kanako Nishi (Shincho Bunko)*
Fuji Diary, Yuriko Takeda (Chuko Bunko)*
Bonjour Tristesse, Françoise Sagan (Penguin Books)
The Girl Next Door, Jack Ketchum (47North)
The Failed Lovers' Suicide at the Falls of Akame, Chokitsu Kurumatani (Bunshun Bunko)*
Never Let Me Go, Kazuo Ishiguro (Faber & Faber)

Afterword

My Life Today, Miri Masuda (Mishimasha)*
Beautiful Distance, Nao-Cola Yamazaki (Bunshun Bunko)*
Without Even Saying Goodbye, Kentaro Ueno (Beam Comics)*

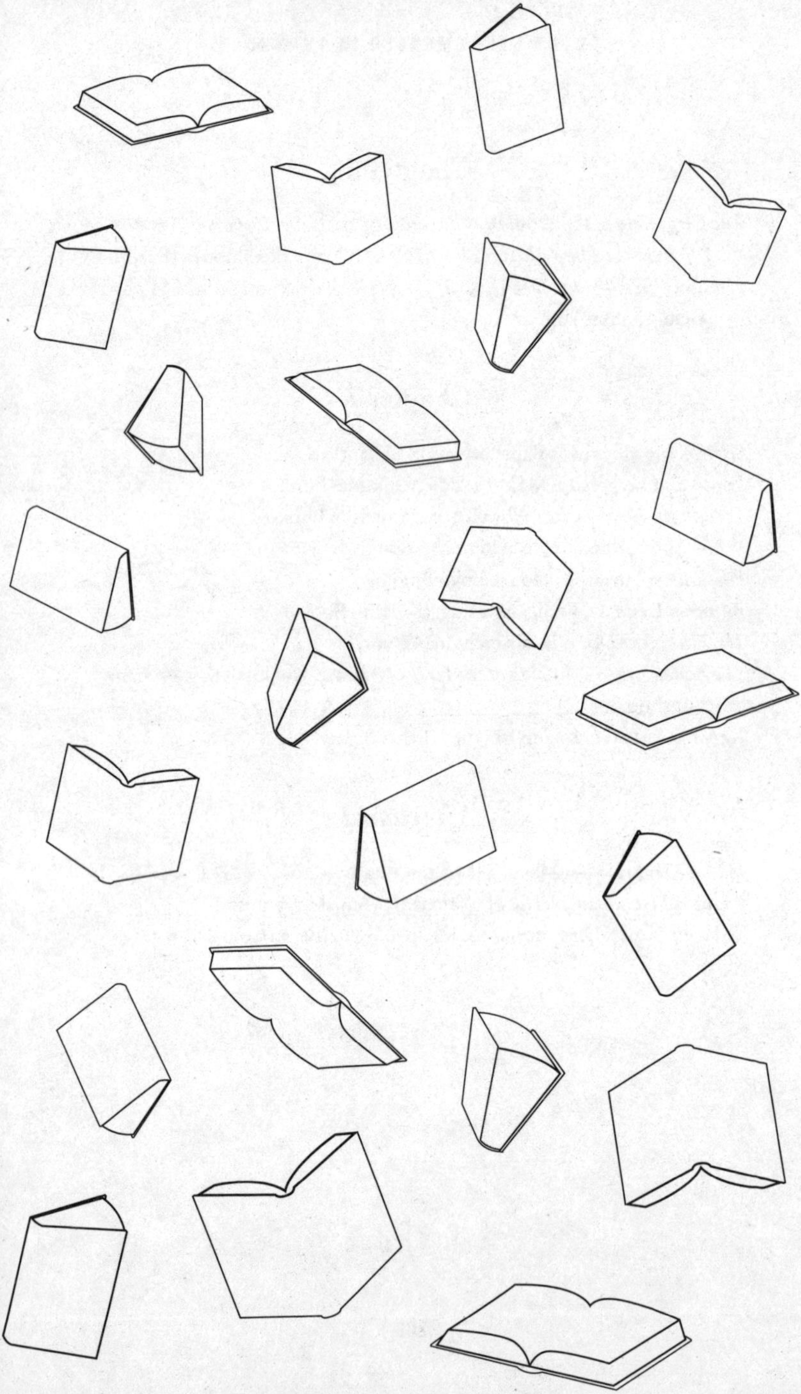

BOOKS RECOMMENDED FOR PEOPLE WHO'VE READ THIS BOOK

Books recommended by Nanako Hanada

Talk to Her, Hirosuke Takaishi (Shobunsha)*
A roman à clef about a young man who repeatedly stops women he doesn't know in the street and speaks to them. It's as though he's training himself – he goes from being a poor communicator to a pick-up artist, breaking new ground in interacting with strangers. A lot of the interactions involve very frank exchanges of coarse sentiments, so it can be a tough read, but it's a unique, fascinating depiction of someone honing his instincts and learning to get a feel for other people. It's also interesting as the author's coming-of-age story, and it was a big motivator for me to try writing about my own experiences in the same way.

*Books with an asterisk are not available in English at time of translation.

***When Strangers Meet: How People You Don't Know Can Transform You*, Kio Stark (Simon & Schuster)**
When Strangers Meet is a sort of proposition that teaches you the merits and enjoyment to be had in exchanging just a few words with strangers in the streets. Having met so many new people myself, a lot of what's said in this book resonates with me. In Japanese society, we're gripped by these negative ideas about people we don't know – *they're scary, they're only after sex, they're stalkers, I'm going to get dragged into some sort of incident* – and reading *When Strangers Meet* really made me want to raise my own voice too, and offer up a different perspective.

Book Revolution in Seoul*, Shintaro Uchinuma and Ayame Yoshinobu (editors), Yukiko Tanaka (photography) (Asahi Press)
Book Revolution in Seoul introduces a number of notable Seoul bookshops. It was through this book that I discovered Jeong Jihye, who offers customers appointments in her bookshop during which they have a chat and she prescribes them a book. I introduced myself to Jihye at an event she did in Japan and we immediately hit it off. My visits to Seoul to meet up with Jihye made me consider my own experiences, and about how sharing them might help other people. They also gave me the cunning plan to write this book before someone else in Japan got there first!

BOOKS RECOMMENDED FOR PEOPLE WHO'VE READ THIS BOOK

Lacklustre Diary*, Mineko Nomachi (Gentosha Bunko)
The protagonist of this comic-book masterpiece is a late bloomer, a twenty-six-year-old virgin with no romantic experience. One day she decides she has to do something about her situation, and the book depicts her tentatively confronting the issues of romance and sex as she gets involved with men on dating sites and at work. There's nothing glaringly outrageous about the story – no problems with a husband's penis that won't fit, no visits to lesbian brothels – so it might look unassuming, but it's so good I think it should be selling in the hundreds of thousands. Nomachi's portrayal of the turbulent emotions of ordinary, fragile people really tugs at the heartstrings, and the scene in chapter 13 of her protagonist standing alone in the subway station after falling out with a colleague is just too painful; I cry every time I read it. The way Nomachi captures her characters' feelings is just perfect.

Wine, Dine and Woo Me*, Nayuka Miné (Fusosha)
And now something totally different: a collection of light-hearted, entertaining manga essays. Miné dines out in a variety of restaurants, each time accompanied by a different man who's been selected through an application process, and the two experience the joys of conversing for the first time. I think there are some really interesting, unique observations and insights here. What struck me more than anything was the way Miné and her date sound each other out as they move the conversation

forward, which was very like what I experienced first hand on PerfectStrangers. I recommend this book to anyone who's wondering how you actually talk to a stranger when you're meeting with just the two of you.

It Chooses You, **Miranda July (Canongate)**
A collection of interviews, again on the theme of encountering strangers. Even in this digital age, there are still some intriguing people who use classified-ads papers to sell their unwanted things. July goes to meet these people in person and try to find out what they're like. The strangers' stories are vivid and unedited, and July doesn't polish them to make them easier to understand. She discovers that going face to face with other people's stories is like taking a closer look at yourself, which is something I found too, thinking back on my own experiences.

My Lesbian Experience with Loneliness, **Kabi Nagata, translated by Jocelyne Allen (Seven Seas)**
When I started writing down my own real-life experiences, I got interested in finding out what other authors had written about in similar popular autobiographies. Nagata's circumstances and her way of thinking were totally different from mine, but reading over her manga monologues again after now having experienced writing about myself, I get a sense of how, despite being in a really tough situation, she persisted in digging down deep inside and facing up to the ugly parts of herself, and how she kept on fighting. I like fighters.

BOOKS RECOMMENDED FOR PEOPLE WHO'VE READ THIS BOOK

Unbearable, Ichiko Uemoto (Taba Books)*
I've always been a keen reader of Ichiko's books, and I've been lucky enough to talk to her and get to know her in person. When writing my own true story, I was initially hesitant about portraying real people in a negative light and revealing my true feelings. I spoke to Ichiko about this, and something she said suddenly made me realise what it was I wanted to aim for; it was like she opened a door for me. *Unbearable* is a book I've held dear for a long time as being a model of what it is to write about yourself.

Those Times at Gaké Shobo, Kenji Yamashita (Natsuhasha)*
A book written by Kenji Yamashita of Gaké Shobo, the bookshop that appears in my own story (the shop has since moved premises and is now called Hohohoza). Even just in the book's opening, you'll get a good sense of Yamashita's classy, easy-going, yet eccentric-at-heart personality. We've been good friends ever since our first meeting, which I wrote about in this book – and of all my betters in the world of bookshops, he's still the one I respect the most. He makes me want to stay a loser, to stay uncool.

Books recommended by Brazen

The Nakano Thrift Shop, Hiromi Kawakami, translated by Allison Markin Powell (Granta Books)
Like Nanako, protagonist Hitomi hasn't gone down a typical company career path, instead choosing to work in a quirky thrift

shop with a cast of eccentric characters. She's also drifting through life a little, and the story is underpinned by her anxiety about change, and about what we want in our relationships with others – both things that are explored in *The Bookshop Woman* too.

***There's No Such Thing as an Easy Job*, Kikuko Tsumura, translated by Polly Barton (Bloomsbury)**
Another book involving unconventional career paths: the protagonist moves from one offbeat workplace to another, helped along now and then by supportive colleagues, as she tries to understand what it is she really wants from her work.

***Dear Reader: The Comfort and Joy of Books*, Cathy Rentzenbrink (Picador)**
This is Cathy Rentzenbrink's memoir, intertwined with the books that have meant the most to her. Cathy follows a similar path to Nanako, starting out on the bookshop floor and then growing more confident in herself and her abilities. Like Nanako, books are a key part of her identity and see her through the highs and lows of life; and like Nanako, she finds a way to help people through books. If Nanako's story resonates with you, *Dear Reader* will too and you'll end up with even more book recommendations.

BOOKS RECOMMENDED FOR PEOPLE WHO'VE READ THIS BOOK

Hyperbole and a Half, Allie Brosh (Square Peg)
Allie Brosh's intentionally crudely-drawn cartoons were an internet hit, and several sections of this book started out life on her blog. She covers everyday life with her dogs, as well as some tough topics – her depiction of what it feels like to have depression has been highly praised. Her use of humour and cartoons to describe quite heavy themes is something we see in some of the titles Nanako recommends.

Inlands, Elin Willows, translated by Duncan J Lewis (Nordisk Books)
Like Nanako's own story, this book begins with a house move and the end of a relationship. Having relocated to a tiny community near the Arctic Circle, the protagonist struggles with her loneliness as well as her freedom.

Diary of a Tuscan Bookshop, Alba Donati, translated by Elena Pala (Weidenfeld & Nicolson)
This is the memoir of a poet who runs a bookshop in Italy. After a career in publishing, Alba crowd-funded her bookshop (like Nanako's own current bookshop in Tokyo), which is set up on a hill in a tiny, idyllic-sounding Tuscan village. Alba talks a lot about the books she loves and notes down what people buy – so again, you end up with lots of great recommendations.

This **brazen** book was created by:

Publisher: Romilly Morgan
Senior Editor: Leanne Bryan
Editorial Assistant: Elise Solberg
Creative Director & Cover Designer: Mel Four
Copyeditor: Joanna Smith
Typesetter: Jouve
Production Manager: Caroline Alberti
Sales: Lucy Helliwell
Publicity & Marketing: Hazel O'Brien, Charlotte Sanders
    & Rosa Patel
Legal: Sasha Duszynska Lewis, Imogen Plouviez
    & Reviewed & Cleared